Shakespeare
THE
KING JAMES
VERSION

Shakespeare
THE KING JAMES VERSION

IAN STOCKDALE

Duke of Dark Corners Publications
Burnaby, British Columbia

Copyright © 2015 Ian Stockdale
All rights reserved.

ISBN 978-0-9948624-2-6 (Electronic Edition)
ISBN 978-0-9948624-1-9 (Paperback Edition)
ISBN 978-0-9948624-0-2 (Hardback Edition)

Editing by Dania Sheldon
Book Design by Glenna Collett

Published by Duke of Dark Corners Publications
Burnaby, British Columbia, Canada
istockda@ianstockdale.com

Visit ianstockdale.com

For Naomi

From my earliest days I have been addicted to the literary arts.

—James VI & I

Acknowledgments

The author wishes to thank the following people for their help and support during the writing of this book: Peter Bowmar, Elva Abdul Hadi, Naomi Inglehart, Tania Paquin, Gina Stockdale, and Robert Van den Ouden.

Contents

Preface — XIII

ONE | Introduction — 1

TWO | King James — 17

THREE | The Evidence — 97

FOUR | The Works — 125

FIVE | Conclusion — 157

APPENDIX 1 | Three Sonnets Dedicated to Tycho Brahe — 163

APPENDIX 2 | The Phoenix and the Turtle — 167

APPENDIX 3 | Timeline — 170

Bibliography — 175

Index — 179

Power never takes a back step—only in the face of more power.
—Malcolm X

Preface

IT WAS THE WINTER OF 2013, and I was watching the second episode of the BBC documentary *Simon Schama's Shakespeare*. The introduction had arrested my attention:

> The question of who kings and queens truly are obsessed the greatest dramatist of all time. In many of Shakespeare's greatest plays kings and queens stalk across the stage: grandiose, bloody-minded, demented, sociopathic. And the question Shakespeare asks of them more insistently, more deeply, more tragically than anyone before or since is this: what happens when a human puts on the crown? Can they be just like us and not at all like us? What happens when the human animal breaks through the mask of royalty?
>
> . . .
>
> Shakespeare's plays were performed right in front of Elizabeth I and her successor James. There they sat in their finery watching stage versions of themselves murder their way

to the throne, go mad, and get turned into pitiful creatures. Shakespeare must have thrived on the thrill of it. Having his actor-kings say the unsayable in front of real-life monarchs. He probed deeper into the royal mind than anyone before or since; exploring the great themes of power, war, and death. From that exploration of kingship, Shakespeare revealed the darkest truths, not just about them, but about us too. (Schama & BBC, 2012)

Thus drawn into this exploration of kingship, I watched as Elizabeth I's reign during the defeat of the Spanish Armada was compared to Shakespeare's *Henry V*, and the queen herself to its eponymous protagonist. The programme then turned to the events of an attempted *coup d'état*, known as the Essex Rebellion, wherein the Earl of Essex and his supporters attempted to turn Elizabeth into a puppet queen and install Essex as the puppetmaster. The night before the failed *coup*, the conspirators had paid for a private showing of Shakespeare's *Richard II*, which dramatizes the deposition of the titular king. After explaining that the rebellion had failed and the ringleaders were executed, Schama mused, 'Shakespeare lived in an age when writing was a dangerous game. Christopher Marlowe was murdered. Thomas Kyd was tortured. Ben Jonson was thrown into jail. So what about Shakespeare? After the Essex Rebellion, could the writer of *Richard II* be had up as an accessory to high treason?' Good question.

The answer given by Michael Boyd, Artistic Director of the Royal Shakespeare Company, was:

> It was a dangerous dance, there's no doubt about it, and you had to become as good with antithesis and metaphor as Shakespeare did, to ski along that razor blade. The reason that

Shakespeare managed to stay out of jail and got his plays onstage and the reason Shakespeare escaped the lesser role of essayist and commentator on the times and achieved the role of the greatest dramatist ever was that he dramatized opposing positions in a way that it is almost impossible to nail him down. (Schama & BBC, 2012)

WTF?

In my experience, and with apologies to Mr. Boyd, power doesn't take a back step in the face of literary antithesis and metaphor, regardless of its brilliance. After all, the long and sordid history of state control of art and artists can hardly be described as illustrative of a fair-minded sensitivity to fine distinctions, can it? Not even at the best of times. But this was not the best of times. It was, as we had just been reminded, 'an age when writing was a dangerous game'. And the play had been performed just before an attempted rebellion, for the rebels! It simply didn't make sense.

My point here is not to pick on Schama and his guest. It is puzzling that Shakespeare escaped from the clutches of Elizabeth's henchmen scot-free when so many of his contemporaries did not. What's more, it generally took far less than a connection to an attempted rebellion to provoke the ire of the Tudor state. Shakespeare's impunity cries out for an explanation. Given the mainstream prohibition on questioning that Shakespeare was undoubtedly a commoner from the small Warwickshire town of Stratford-upon-Avon, Boyd's explanation is just as good as any, I suppose. I do not abide prohibitions on my thought, however.

The whole question reminded me of a theory I'd encountered, that 'Shakespeare' was actually a pseudonym used by someone else, usually believed by the theory's proponents to be a nobleman. I'd seen the *Frontline* documentary *Much Ado About Something* a number of years before, which laid out the problems with the orthodox story regarding 'William Shakespeare'. (Rubbo & McDonald, 2001) Although I'd been struck at the time by how surprisingly unsatisfactory was the answer given by the defenders of the orthodox story, I'd not really followed up on the question further. The so-called Shakespeare Authorship Question certainly hadn't been front of mind when I'd sat down to watch 'Hollow Crowns' that evening. But it was now front and centre as I watched the programme deal with the remaining few years of Elizabeth's life and then begin to describe the opening events of the reign of her successor, James VI and I.

The narrator proceeded to describe what is believed to have been the first performance of a Shakespeare play for James, at Hampton Court, during the 1603 Christmas season. Schama explained, '[W]e don't know exactly what plays were performed that Christmas but it seems very likely that for the King and his Danish queen, it would have been the Danish play—Hamlet. Where else had they spent their honeymoon but Elsinore Castle?' Reviewing certain plot points of *Hamlet*, Schama declared:

> James would have loved the melodrama, but as Hamlet unfolded he must have felt increasingly ill at ease because what James was watching was a reflection of his own life played out on stage. His father, Darnley, had been murdered. The murderer, Bothwell, had married James's mother, Mary, Queen of Scots. They lived as King and Queen, flaunting their crime like Claudius and Gertrude. This nightmare haunted James and here it was again played out right in front of him. (Schama & BBC, 2012)

This was the final straw. What sort of suicidal maniac would present an early seventeenth-century king with a play that would make the monarch 'ill at ease'? Surely only a madman would, 'in an age when writing was a dangerous game', re-enact the life events that constituted the 'nightmare' that haunted the one man with the absolute power to order his torture and killing. What's more, he got away with it. Again.

I tried to make sense of all this and watch the show at the same time. Eventually, I managed to come to the following thought:

'Hmm. Maybe Shakespeare was actually James himself...'.

I was able to watch the remainder of the programme in peace, having decided to check it out afterwards. Later that night, I searched the Internet for answers and discovered that I was not the first person to suspect James's involvement. I found out that none other than Malcolm X had proposed it in his autobiography, published posthumously in 1965, a number of months after his assassination. I was able, with ease, to find online the few paragraphs he devoted to the idea. I then searched, in vain, for any well-reasoned arguments against the candidature, finding only a handful of comments—these being of the quality typical of comments that one tends to find online. To my great surprise, the Internet had been unable to provide me with a satisfactory answer to my question.

I widened my search to the holdings of the library at the University of British Columbia, trying to find evidence that would tend to disprove this theory that James was the true author of the works of Shakespeare, focussing at first on the facts surrounding James and his life. I naturally assumed, initially, that I would fairly quickly find some good reasons why this ridiculous notion wasn't true, and that I would be able to move on with the rest of my life. This was not to be.

The truth is, I knew astonishingly little about the man. I don't particularly blame myself for this lack of knowledge. King James, despite his rank as the fourth-longest reigning monarch in British history,[1] is virtually invisible to our modern culture. This relative invisibility persists despite the fact that his immediate predecessor in Scotland – his mother, Mary, Queen of Scots – is a well-known figure, and his immediate predecessor in England, Elizabeth I, is nothing less than a historical superstar. One of the strange things about this invisibility is that his life, it seems to me, is at least as fascinating as the lives of his mother and his cousin Elizabeth.

The cultural association with Shakespeare is a particularly good example of this strange phenomenon. Unquestionably, Shakespeare is associated in our culture with Elizabeth to an astronomically greater extent than with James, despite the fact that so many of the plays that are overwhelmingly regarded as among his greatest (e.g., *Othello*, *King Lear*, *Macbeth*, *The Tempest*) date from James's reign.[2]

The more I looked into the life of James, the more unlikely it seemed that I would disprove my theory. Indeed, the more I compared James's life to the works of Shakespeare, and vice versa, the more the evidence seemed to suggest that the two subjects were inextricably linked.

---

[1] Including both his reign in Scotland and his reign over England and Scotland.

[2] Although, amazingly enough, *Hamlet* does not—it was unequivocally written *before* James became King of England. This fact was not mentioned in 'Hollow Crowns', and I was unaware of it until I began my research.

It is easy to imagine a farmer's boy emigrating to London and becoming a successful actor and theatre owner; but for him to have become the great poet and dramatist, and to have had such knowledge of foreign courts, cardinals and kings, is inconceivable to me. . . . I can hardly think it was the Stratford boy. Whoever wrote them had an aristocratic attitude.
—Charlie Chaplin

ONE | **Introduction**

D<small>ID YOU KNOW</small> that in the plays of Shakespeare, lines spoken by commoners are almost always written in prose, while lines spoken by noblemen are written in poetry? It's true. Shakespeare, whoever he was, had utter contempt for us commoners. Just look at the names he gave to common folk – e.g., Bottom, Elbow, Robert Shallow, Mistress Quickly, Simple (yes, 'Simple' is the name of a character in *Merry Wives of Windsor*). These characters are actually among the privileged few commoners to have been given names; often, Shakespeare couldn't be bothered, and characters are simply called 'a porter' or 'an old shepherd'. In *Julius Caesar*, he dispenses with such differentiation entirely and just gives them each a number: 'commoner #1', 'commoner #2'.

It's not just that we're given disrespectful names or prohibited from speaking any of the quotable lines. Common folk in a Shakespeare play are usually there to be mocked. Time and again in the plays, comic relief is provided by a commoner's malapropism, the character's dim-witted misunderstanding of the situation, or sometimes simply his or her sheer country-bumpkinness. The writer is not laughing *with* us when presenting characters such as Dogberry, the bumbling, self-important nightwatchman from *Much Ado About Nothing* who is constantly spouting malapropisms. He's laughing *at* us.

That's a bit rich coming from the son of a farmer-turned-glover from provincial Warwickshire, isn't it? Where does he get off?

Nobody seriously doubts that a man with a name approximating William Shakspere (alternately spelled Shacksper, Shakspere, Shaxper, or possibly Shagspere, among others) was born, raised, and eventually died in Stratford-upon-Avon. At the age of 18, he married a woman named Anne Hathaway, had two daughters, Susanna and Judith, and a son, Hamnet, the last of whom died at age eleven. He went to London in the early 1590s, at some point became a 'sharer' (i.e., shareholder) in the playing company The Lord Chamberlain's Men (which later became The King's Men), then retired to his home town in 1613 as a rather wealthy man. He died in 1616, bequeathing to Anne Hathaway his second-best bed. There's nothing controversial about all of that (other than the meaning and significance of the second-best bed bequest, perhaps).

The heart of the controversy is scepticism that it was this William Shakspere who wrote the plays and poems attributed to William Shakespeare. This controversy has arisen because the more we have learned about the works of Shakespeare, and the more we have learned (or been unable to learn) about the life of this man from Stratford, the more incompatible they seem. Serious doubts arose when people went searching for the genius of Shakespeare in the life of William Shakspere and found little of it in the scraps of evidence that surfaced as England was scoured over the centuries for anything that might be connected to Shakspere. Among the things that don't add up are:

1. Close study of the works has revealed that the author writes from a ruling-class point of view and displays expert, insider knowledge of court life, along with ruling-class sports and pastimes, inconsistent with Shakspere's upbringing.
2. The author displays a huge vocabulary and vast education in a diverse range of subjects, including a knowledge of languages not taught at the local grammar school in Stratford, such as French, Spanish, and Italian.
3. The sublime poet doesn't seem to match the mundane, businesslike, penny-pinching Stratford man the evidence shows him to be.
4. His parents and both of his daughters were illiterate, marking 'x' on legal documents.
5. The only examples of Shakspere's handwriting that anyone has been able to find are six messy signatures.
6. No evidence from during his lifetime has ever been found supporting the claim that he was an author; only posthumously was he ever referred to as one.

These doubts form the basis for what has become known as the Shakespeare Authorship Question. The contention was and is that the name 'William Shakespeare' was a pseudonym, hiding the identity of the author, or authors, who wished to remain anonymous. Starting in the nineteenth century, people began looking for and considering suitable candidates for the true author. They assumed that a suitable candidate would possess the background, education, and life experience displayed in the plays and poems. From this assumption, a suitable candidate would likely be a nobleman, or at least someone who had a university education (e.g., had attended Oxford or Cambridge). They also assumed that the person(s) would have had one or more reasons to hide behind a pseudonym.

One of the reasons often given for any candidate drawn from the nobility is something usually referred to as the 'stigma of print'. This stigma was one of the myriad social conventions used to keep the strictly hierarchical world of sixteenth-century Europe strictly hierarchical. The nobility were supposed to live off the work of others, not do any of it themselves. To publish anything, let alone something as grubby as a play, in the marketplace to be bought and sold for profit was therefore frowned upon as common.

The first serious candidate to emerge was English philosopher, scientist, jurist, and statesman Sir Francis Bacon, when it was noticed that the works of Shakespeare contain allusions to Baconian philosophy and concepts, along with legal knowledge and parallels with Bacon's life. However, Bacon wasn't a nobleman, and the stigma of print didn't apply to him. He was, indeed, a noted author of various books printed in his lifetime.

Another major candidate has been Christopher Marlowe, playwright of the Elizabethan theatrical smash hit *The Jew of Malta*, as well as *Tamburlaine the Great*, *Doctor Faustus*, and other plays. Proponents of the Marlovian theory contend that Marlowe faked his own death to avoid accusations of Catholic intrigue and/or atheism. This theory is helped by the fact that the poem *Venus and Adonis*, the first hit by 'William Shakespeare', was published one week after Marlowe's apparent death under suspicious circumstances in a Deptford tavern. Marlowe's candidacy is at the heart of the *Frontline* documentary *Much Ado About Something* as well as Ros Barber's recent novel *The Marlowe Papers*.

By far and away the most popular candidate for almost 100 years has been Edward de Vere, 17th Earl of Oxford. Oxford was first proposed as a candidate by J. Thomas Looney, in his 1920 book *'Shakespeare' Identified*. Looney identified eighteen characteristics of the author of the works, such as knowledge of Italy and Italian. He then sought candidates who fit the characteristics, deciding that the (at the time) obscure de Vere was the best fit.

De Vere, Marlowe, and Bacon are the 'big three' candidates for Shakespeare authorship, but many more have been proposed over the years – more than eighty, in fact, although at least a few of these have been more tongue-in-cheek than serious proposals.

As I mentioned in the Preface, Malcolm X proposed King James as the true author, devoting a scant three paragraphs to the entire Shakespeare Authorship Question. Describing his time in prison in the 1940s and the various intellectual debates in which he engaged while there, he wrote:

> Another hot debate I remember I was in had to do with the identity of Shakespeare. No color was involved there; I just got intrigued over the Shakespearean dilemma. The King James translation of the Bible is considered the greatest piece of literature in English. Its language supposedly represents the

ultimate in using the King's English. Well, Shakespeare's language and the Bible's language are one and the same. They say that from 1604 to 1611, King James got poets to translate, to write the Bible. Well, if Shakespeare existed, he was then the top poet around. But Shakespeare is nowhere reported connected with the Bible. If he existed, why didn't King James use him? And if he did use him, why is it one of the world's best kept secrets?

I know that many say that Francis Bacon was Shakespeare. If that is true, why would Bacon have kept it secret? Bacon wasn't royalty, when royalty sometime used the nom de plume because it was 'improper' for royalty to be artistic or theatrical. What would Bacon have had to lose? Bacon, in fact, would have had everything to gain.

In the prison debates I argued for the theory that King James himself was the real poet who used the nom de plume Shakespeare. King James was brilliant. He was the greatest king who ever sat on the British throne. Who else among royalty, in his time, would have had the giant talent to write Shakespeare's works? It was he who poetically 'fixed' the Bible – which in itself and its present King James version has enslaved the world. (X & Haley, 1965, p. 185)

Sure, we can quibble with some of brother Malcolm's claims. For instance, the British clearly didn't enslave the world with the King James Version of the Bible; they did so primarily with redcoats and Royal Navy gunboats. Nevertheless, those prison debates must have been *extraordinary*.

Malcolm X was not the only well-known person to doubt the identity of Shakespeare. Some notable doubters include Sigmund Freud, Henry James, William James, Charles Dickens,

Ralph Waldo Emerson, Walt Whitman, Charlie Chaplin, and Mark Twain. Mark Twain devoted an entire chapter of his autobiography to the question. He had visited Stratford-upon-Avon during his travels in Europe, and the visit helped to convince him that it was not the birthplace of the actual author of the works of Shakespeare. Twain (actually Samuel Clemens, writing under the pseudonym of Mark Twain) compares his own experience of growing up in the small, backwater town of Hannibal, Missouri. He notes the paucity of evidence that, during and shortly after the death of William Shakspere, the townsfolk of Stratford knew or cared that a celebrated poet and playwright had grown up in their midst. This was in direct contrast to his experience with the townsfolk of Hannibal's remembrance of their favourite son. He compares what is actually known and can be proven about William Shakspere with what has been conjectured by biographers, and concludes: 'All the rest of his vast history, as furnished by the biographers, is built up, course upon course, of guesses, inferences, theories, conjectures – an Eiffel Tower of artificialities rising sky-high from a very flat and very thin foundation of inconsequential facts' (Twain, 1991, p. 418).

Throughout this book, the name 'Shakspere' will be used to refer to the man born and raised in Stratford, while 'Shakespeare' will always be used to refer to the author, whoever that may be, of the works of William Shakespeare.

What I will refer to in this book as 'The Stratfordian position', and those who hold this position as 'Stratfordians', accept the proposition that William Shakspere was the author. Stratfordians start from the fact that the name 'William Shakespeare' appeared on a number of plays and poems during Shakspere's lifetime. The name 'William Shakespeare' also appears on the

First Folio, which was published in 1623, seven years after Shakspere's death. The First Folio contains a dedicatory poem by Ben Jonson, wherein Jonson calls Shakespeare 'the soul of the age' as well as 'Sweet Swan of Avon'. The Avon is, of course, the river flowing through Stratford-upon-Avon. A writer named Leonard Digges refers to 'thy Stratford monument'. Two actors from the King's Men (the acting company in which Shakspere was a shareholder), John Heminges and William Condell, ostensibly the compilers of the volume, lent their names to the First Folio as well. Stratfordians also point to certain lines, images, or allusions which they claim display evidence of such things as knowledge of the tanning trade (related to Shakspere's father's glove-making trade), and being raised both in the countryside and in and around Shakspere's native Warwickshire.

I have no desire to set up any straw men with respect to the Stratfordian position. However, it would be inaccurate to omit the argument, often employed by Stratfordians, that anyone who doubts is a classist snob. Indeed, that 'argument' turns up so regularly that it could reasonably be described as their 'go-to' tactic. Just type 'Shakespeare authorship snobbery' into your search engine of choice and behold the results. Take, for example, a website called 'RationalWiki', which contains the following on its 'Shakespeare Authorship' page, reached via the 'Conspiracy Theories Portal' (presumably pursuant to one of the wiki's stated purposes, to 'document the full range of crank ideas'): 'Historically, the case against Shakespeare's authorship is grounded in certain prejudices held by his readership' ("Shakespeare authorship," n.d.).

This is simply sophistry, obviously.

Such an argument is called an *ad hominem* (Latin for 'to the person') argument. In a case of delicious irony, RationalWiki also has a page devoted to explaining that type of fallacy, which it does efficiently:

> an ad hominem argument occurs when one attacks the person making an argument rather than the argument itself. It is therefore a special case of the broader category of formal logical fallacies, the non sequitur, in which the conclusion urged, e.g. that the disputant is incorrect, does not follow from the premise asserted, e.g. that the disputant is a dick. Even if the ad hominem attack is true, that fact has no bearing on whether the disputant's argument is logically sound. ("Argumentum ad hominem," n.d.)

At the risk of insulting the reader's intelligence by pointing out the obvious, Mark Twain, Charlie Chaplin, Charles Dickens, and Malcolm X could not be worse examples of classist snobs. Not only does the premise that doubters are snobs have absolutely no bearing on the soundness of the doubters' arguments but, as the above examples demonstrate, it is undeniably false. If anything, doubt regarding the identity of Shakespeare seems to be negatively correlated with class snobbery. But the result is the same even if one uses an example in which the premise is true. For example, HRH Prince Philip, Duke of Edinburgh, has recently come out as a Shakespeare Authorship doubter. Philip, who reportedly once commented to vicious Paraguayan dictator Alfredo Stroessner on what a pleasure it was 'to be in a country that isn't ruled by its people' (Rudd, 2013), is, perhaps, the quintessential classist snob. Note that the truth or falsity of the assertion that the works of Shakespeare were not written by William Shakspere of Stratford remains exactly the same whether it comes out of the mouth of Prince Philip or of the Little Tramp himself.

The Stratfordian position actually has what could be described as an official spokes-organization, called the Shakespeare Birthplace Trust (SBT). Whether or not the SBT speaks for all Stratfordians, I don't know, but the SBT claims that there is no room for doubt regarding the Shakespeare Authorship Question: William Shakspere and William Shakespeare were one and the same person, end of story. Remarkably, the SBT takes the further position that this absence of doubt implies that no one else should enquire further into the question. They actively discourage enquiry.

It is in the face of such organized resistance to freedom of thought regarding the Shakespeare Authorship Question that an organization called the Shakespeare Authorship Coalition (SAC) was created. The SAC is a non-profit organization which, while not advocating for any particular alternative authorship candidate, is 'dedicated to legitimizing the Shakespeare authorship issue by increasing awareness of reasonable doubt about the identity of William Shakespeare'. To that end, the SAC have created the 'Declaration of Reasonable Doubt About the Identity of William Shakespeare'. It states: 'We, the undersigned, hereby declare our view that there *is* room for reasonable doubt about the identity of William Shakespeare, and that it is an important question for anyone seeking to understand the works, the formative literary culture in which they were produced, or the nature of literary creativity and genius' (The Shakespeare Authorship Coalition, 2015). It lays out the best evidence for the proposition that the identity of William Shakespeare is William Shakspere and then rebuts each piece of evidence, point by point. The SAC invites people to sign the Declaration of Reasonable Doubt, at www.doubtaboutwill.org. At the time of writing, the Declaration had 3,175 signatures. One of those signatures is mine, signed on 2 April 2013.

The plays and poems not only have a consistent ruling-class point of view but are imbued with references to aristocratic sports, leisure activities, and class-specific concerns, such as titles and honour. It is this preoccupation with honour that struck Charlie Chaplin, who remarked:

> I dislike Shakespearean themes involving kings, queens, august people and their honour. Perhaps it is something psychological within me, possibly my peculiar solipsism. In my pursuit of bread and cheese, honour was seldom trafficked in. I cannot identify myself with a prince's problems. (Chaplin, 1964, p. 275)

Chaplin, like Twain, had actually visited Stratford-upon-Avon. Also like Twain, his visit helped to foster the scepticism he had regarding the authorship of the Shakespeare corpus. With respect to Stratford, he said: 'That such a mind ever dwelt or had its beginnings there seems incredible. . . . In the work of the greatest of geniuses humble beginnings will reveal themselves somewhere – but one cannot trace the slightest sign of them'.

The showstopper for me is the fact that both of Shakspere's daughters made a 'mark' when signing legal documents, a sure sign of illiteracy. What sort of Talibanesque monster was William Shakspere to have written works of such literary transcendence yet forbid his daughters from learning even the basics of the language? Perhaps it had nothing to do with gender; maybe he simply hated or supremely resented his offspring. But if he hated his children or simply didn't care about them at all, why then did he give the bulk of his estate to them in his will? There's no evidence whatever that they suffered from any physical or mental disability that would have prevented them from learning to read. It just doesn't add up.

For Stratfordians to not recognize the importance of Shakspere's daughters' illiteracy is doubly incomprehensible when one considers that so many Stratfordians are professors of English literature. How does one who has dedicated his or her life to the study of the English language explain that one of its greatest practitioners did not share his life's work with his children? Shakspere's daughters most likely never read a single sonnet written by William Shakespeare, let alone *Hamlet*, or any other play, for that matter. It's unbelievable, really. I'm genuinely curious whether there is anything even a little bit plausible to explain how a situation like that could have arisen. I'm not aware of anyone even attempting an explanation. This inconvenient fact, like so many others surrounding the Shakespeare mystery, is simply ignored by Stratfordians.

Just think, for a moment, what the Stratfordian position entails. William Shakspere was born into and raised in an illiterate household, with neither parent able to teach him to read. He attends the Stratford grammar school, learns to read, and eventually is the greatest writer of all time, becoming rather wealthy in the process. He then decides to end this whole experiment with reading and writing in the Shakspere family and neither teaches his kids to write nor even arranges for them to be taught. Stratfordians are asking us to believe that the sixteenth-century family tree of the Shakspere of Stratford-upon-Avon, if you counted down generation by generation, went something like this: illiterate, illiterate, illiterate, greatest writer of all time, illiterate. . . .

The Curious Incidence of Documentary Evidence

An invaluable resource for anyone wishing to take an objective look at the Shakespeare Authorship Question is Diana Price's *Shakespeare's Unorthodox Biography: New Evidence of an Authorship Problem*. Price has made no claim regarding any particular candidate for the identity of the author. Blowing away the considerable smoke that has been generated from the thousands (millions?) of words of orthodox biography of Shakespeare written over hundreds of years, Price examined the hard evidence that exists with respect to William Shakspere of Stratford to find what evidence actually links him with being a professional writer.

Following this 'literary paper trail', as she calls it, Price looked for documentary evidence sorted into ten separate categories:

1. Evidence of education
2. Record of correspondence, especially concerning literary matters
3. Evidence of having been paid to write
4. Evidence of a direct relationship with a patron
5. Extant original manuscript(s)
6. Handwritten inscriptions, receipts, letters, etc. touching on literary matters
7. Commendatory verses, epistles, or epigrams contributed or received
8. Miscellaneous records (e.g., referred to personally as a writer)
9. Evidence of books owned, written in, borrowed, or given
10. Notice at death as a writer (dated up to twelve months following death to allow for eulogies or reports of death)

How many categories did Shakspere tally in? Zero. Price found, in fact, that there was no hard, unambiguous, documentary evidence of any sort to link him, in his lifetime (or at his death), to a career as a writer. Nothing. What's more, she was able to find at least one piece of evidence in no fewer than three categories for all of the other familiar (and some not-so-familiar) names associated with Elizabethan and Jacobean drama. Price collected data on twenty-five early modern English writers of the period.

Ben Jonson scored a perfect ten (i.e., at least one piece of evidence in all ten categories), the only writer to do so. Thomas Nashe came in second with nine categories (missing only notice at death as a writer). Edmund Spenser and George Chapman each scored a seven. John Marston, Thomas Middleton, John Lyly, Thomas Heywood, Thomas Lodge, and Robert Greene have evidence in six categories. Thomas Dekker had five. Near the bottom of the pack, Christopher Marlowe, Francis Beaumont, John Fletcher, and Thomas Kyd scored in only four categories. In fact, only two of the twenty-five writers that Price analysed had at least one piece of evidence in fewer than four categories: John Webster, who had three and Shakspere, with the aforementioned goose egg (Price, 2001, pp. 301–313).

It is not surprising that there are gaps in the evidentiary record for these early modern playwrights. For one thing, roughly four centuries have passed. Furthermore, the Puritans closed and banned the English theatres near the middle of the seventeenth century. The Great Fire of London, in 1666, undoubtedly destroyed many documents. It's perhaps lucky that we have as much of the record as we do. What's clear from Diana Price's research, though, is that Shakspere is the only playwright of the period for whom the evidentiary record tying that person to the works attributed to him is a completely blank slate.

That this blank slate should be associated with Shakespeare is *ridiculously* strong evidence of an authorship problem when one considers the amount of human effort, a great deal of it scholarly, that has been directed towards researching this one playwright compared to all other twenty-four combined. As Oxford historian Hugh Trevor-Roper wrote:

> Of all the immortal geniuses of literature, none is personally so elusive as William Shakespeare. It is exasperating, and almost incredible, that he should be so. After all, he lived in the full daylight of the English Renaissance, in the well-documented reigns of Queen Elizabeth and King James I. He wrote thirty-five plays and 150 highly personal sonnets. He was connected with some of the best-known public figures in the most conspicuous court in English history. Since his death, particularly in the last century, he has been subjected to the greatest battery of organized research that has ever been directed upon a single person. And yet the greatest of all Englishman, after this tremendous inquisition, still remains so close a mystery that even his identity can still be doubted. (Trevor-Roper, 1962)

Kings Actions, even in the secretest Places, are as the Actions of those that are set upon the Stages.
—King James, speech to Parliament, 21 March 1610

TWO | King James

BIOGRAPHY

THE LIFE STORY OF JAMES STUART bears a striking resemblance to a Shakespeare play. It is filled with ambition, intrigue, revenge, bawdiness, weddings, regime change, male camaraderie, homoeroticism, witches, assorted earls, the occasional duke, and a fateful storm. The relevant facts, laid out in roughly chronological order, are as follows:

PROLOGUE

B Cassiopeiae

Thousands of years ago, in a part of space that we classify as the Cassiopeia constellation, a white dwarf star went supernova. That is, a very dense star at the end of its life cycle (i.e., a white dwarf) combined with the mass of a nearby star, gravitationally increasing its mass and density to the point that it set off a massive thermonuclear explosion that astronomers label a type Ia supernova. Of course, that is our modern, scientific explanation for this distant event. Humanity, which was just reaching the tail end of the Stone Age at the time of the explosion, would remain oblivious to the entire event for thousands of years. However, the light given off by the explosion, when it did finally reach the Earth, would help to overturn centuries of thinking about the cosmos.

The Wars of the Roses (1455–1487) and Their Aftermath

Edward III of England reigned from 1327 to 1377. Edward started a costly, bloody war with France that raged, on and off, for 116 years (1337–1453), euphemistically called the Hundred Years' War. Edward also had a large family, with nine children who survived infancy: five sons and four daughters. Social and financial strains brought about by the Hundred Years' War led Edward III's descendants to break down into two opposing factions, and they fought a costly, bloody civil war that raged, on and off, for thirty-two years (1455–1487), called the Wars of the Roses.

The Wars of the Roses were fought on the pretext of the 'claim to the throne' each side asserted. One's claim to the throne was determined by the rules of primogeniture. The Wikipedia article for 'order of succession' defines primogeniture succinctly:

> In primogeniture (or more precisely male primogeniture) the monarch's eldest son and his descendants take precedence over his siblings and their descendants. Elder sons take precedence over younger sons, but all sons take precedence over all daughters. Children represent their deceased

ancestors, and the senior line of descent always takes precedence over the junior line, within each gender. The right of succession belongs to the eldest son of the reigning monarch, and then to the eldest son. ("Order of succession," n.d.)

Be forewarned, this simple set of rules can lead to some headache-inducing complexity when tracing a claim to the throne back through more than a couple of generations. Indeed, it could be argued that the complexity helped to fuel the Wars of the Roses. Hopefully, we'll keep this as simple as possible.

All of the trouble can be traced back to Edward III's four eldest sons:

1. Edward III's eldest son, known as Edward the Black Prince, fathered a son, Richard, but the Black Prince died before his father, Edward III, did. When Edward III died, his grandson Richard was named King Richard II.
2. Edward III's second son, Lionel of Antwerp, 1st Duke of Clarence, had only one child, a daughter named Philippa. Note how the rules of primogeniture operated to give the crown to Richard, not Lionel, as 'the right of succession belongs to the eldest son of the reigning monarch, and then to the eldest son'. Had Edward the Black Prince died childless, the Crown would have passed to Lionel of Antwerp.
3. Edward III's third son, John of Gaunt, 1st Duke of Lancaster, had four legitimate children: a son, Henry, and three daughters. He also had four children outside of marriage, given the surname 'Beaufort' (not Lancaster), after one of John's possessions in France. John of Gaunt, as 1st Duke of Lancaster, founded what's known as the

House of Lancaster. His descendants made up the House of Lancaster and thus are sometimes referred to as 'Lancastrians'.

4. Edward III's fourth son, Edmund of Langley, 1st Duke of York, had two sons and one daughter. Edmund founded the House of York.

In 1399, John of Gaunt's son, Henry, deposed his cousin Richard to become Henry IV, the first Lancastrian king. His son was Henry V, whose son was Henry VI. Henry VI was named King of England as a nine-month-old baby. He'd inherited not only the crown but the Hundred Years' War that had been started by his great-great-grandfather, Edward III.

Henry's VI's father had started up the fighting again, after a long period of peace. Henry V, through victory after victory, had expanded English territory in France. Further fighting after Henry V's death took English territory in France to its greatest peak around the time that Henry VI was about five or six years old. From that time forward, however, momentum switched to the French side in the war, as the French went from victory to victory, taking back the English gains.

Henry VI was a weak king – timid, overly pious, and suffering from bouts of insanity (he may have had schizophrenia). This weakness, combined with the strains of decades of fighting a war that the English were now losing, led to increasingly bitter factional struggles among the powerful nobles at Henry's court. When the patriarch of the House of York, Richard, 3rd Duke of York, was excluded from government by Lancastrians, he decided to press his claim to the throne. How could a descendant of Edward III's fourth son (Edmund of Langley, 1st Duke of York) justify a claim to the throne over a descendant of Edward III's third son (John of Gaunt, 1st Duke of Lancaster)? Aren't the rules of primogeniture clear that the Duke of York's claim was inferior to Henry VI's? Perhaps, but for one other detail. The Duke of York was also a direct descendant of Lionel of Antwerp, 1st Duke of Clarence, through Lionel's only daughter, Philippa. Oy yoy yoy! How would you decide, in this case, who had the better claim to the throne?

On the field of battle, by test of military strength, that's how. That was, in any event, the preferred method of Richard, 3rd Duke of York. Legalistic claims to the throne were, at the end of the day, never going to trump violence as the ultimate arbiter in questions of this sort, certainly not in the fifteenth century. Yorkist and Lancastrian forces clashed initially in 1455, at the First Battle of St. Albans, a stunning Yorkist victory. Although Richard, Duke of York would never be king (he fell in battle in 1460), his son became Edward IV after the Yorkists took the throne. The Lancastrians were able to win back the throne, reinstating Henry VI, but then lost it again to Edward IV. When Edward IV died, his young son became Edward V for a few months, until Edward IV's brother, Richard, quickly manipulated his way to becoming King Richard III.

Richard III would be the last king from the House of York. Lancastrian forces, led by Henry Tudor, won a decisive victory over Richard III at Bosworth Field, in 1487. The Wars of the Roses were over. Henry Tudor – whose claim to the throne derived from his descent from John of Gaunt, Duke of Lancaster, through John Beaufort, one of the Duke's 'illegitimate' sons – was crowned King Henry VII.[1] Henry Tudor was the first Tudor king. He was the father of Henry VIII, who in turn was the father of Elizabeth I. Elizabeth was crowned, in Westminster Abbey, on 15 January 1559.

---

1. Although the Beauforts had been fathered by John of Gaunt outside of marriage, they weren't legally illegitimate, since they had been legitimated by both papal bull and royal decree in 1396 and 1397, respectively.

The 4th Earl of Bothwell

In 1556, Patrick Hepburn, 3rd Earl of Bothwell and Lord High Admiral of Scotland, died. Consequently, his twenty-one-year-old son, James Hepburn, became, unsurprisingly, the 4th Earl of Bothwell. More surprising to modern eyes, perhaps, was the fact that the lad also became the Lord High Admiral of Scotland, just as his father before him and his father's father before him. After all, it was the olden days, and it made perfect sense that a twenty-one-year-old should simply inherit this title, which gave its holder 'command of the King's ships and sailors and inspection of all sea ports, harbours, and sea coasts', as well as the prerogative to appoint 'judges to decide causes relating to maritime affairs, including both civil and criminal jurisdiction, and jurisdiction over creeks, fresh and navigable waterways' ("Lord High Admiral of Scotland," n.d.).

Pursuant to his duties as Lord High Admiral, the young Bothwell sailed to various ports around Europe. On one of these voyages he met, and married, Anna Throndsen, the daughter of a Norwegian pirate-turned admiral in the Danish navy who, at the time of Bothwell's arrival, was serving as Danish Royal Consul in Copenhagen. The couple left Denmark for Scotland, but Anna swiftly came to realize that Bothwell was a loathsome piece of work. In Flanders, the rascal declared he was out of money and convinced Anna to sell all of her possessions, then to visit her family in Denmark to ask for more funds. He then abandoned her to travel to France.

It was here at the French court, in the summer of 1560, that Bothwell first met Mary, Queen of Scots. At the time, Mary was wedded to the King of France, Francis II. By December of that year, however, Francis II was dead from a mysterious ear condition. Rumours, unsubstantiated to this day, circulated that he had been poisoned. The rumour mongers usually presumed the alleged murder to have been a Protestant plot. After Francis's death, Mary returned to her native Scotland to rule. Despite being a declared Protestant, Bothwell allied himself with the Catholic Mary against the Protestant lords in Scotland. In February 1566, he married Lady Jean Gordon, divorcing her fourteen months later.

Henry Stuart, Lord Darnley

The year earlier, Queen Mary had married Henry Stuart, Lord Darnley. The couple were first cousins, as grandchildren of Margaret Tudor (daughter of England's Henry VII). Although Mary quickly became pregnant, matrimonial happiness was short-lived. Darnley soon turned out to be an immature, vicious, syphilitic drunkard who became jealous of the relationship between the Queen and her private secretary, David Rizzio. The Italian-born Rizzio, a talented fiddler and singer, had quickly worked his way up the ladder of the Queen's servants. Mary's husband wasn't alone in his concern for the closeness of Rizzio's relationship with the Queen. Protestants, in particular, were wary of the growing influence of this ambitious Catholic foreigner.

One night, Queen Mary, then six months pregnant, was dining with Rizzio in her private dining room at Holyrood Palace. A gang of men burst in and carried Rizzio off, stabbing him over fifty times in the process, then tossing him down a flight of stairs. The manner in which this murder was conducted, right in front of the Queen, suggests that the intent of the perpetrators was also to induce a miscarriage. As it happened, Mary did not miscarry, and she gave birth a few months later, on 19 June 1566. Thus was wee James born into the chaotic brutality of sixteenth-century Scotland, having already survived an attempt on his life.

Darnley's jealousy had been stoked by rumours that Rizzio may have been the real father. These rumours persisted into the seventeenth century, and they haunted James. Henry IV of France, referencing the rumours of the musician's paternity while also poking fun at James's self-image as 'Solomon of Scotland', joked that he hoped the Scottish king was not 'Solomon son of David who played upon the harp'. According to Pauline Croft, 'As a child James wept in mortification at [the rumours], and in 1600 a hostile Scottish mob shouted at him "Come down thou son of Seigneur Davy"' (Croft, 2003, p. 11).

Darnley himself was murdered the following February, his body found with signs of strangulation in the orchard of a former abbey that shortly beforehand had been blown to pieces. Suspicion for this murder immediately fell upon James Hepburn, 4th Earl of Bothwell, and his cronies. Over time, rumours started implicating Mary herself, due to what some perceived as a lackadaisical approach to finding the perpetrators. Indeed, Mary's cousin Elizabeth I wrote to her, concerning the rumours:

> I should ill fulfil the office of a faithful cousin or an affectionate friend if I did not . . . tell you what the world is thinking. Men say that, instead of seizing the murderers, you are looking through your fingers while they escape; that you will not seek revenge on those who have done you so much pleasure, as though the deed would never have taken place had not the doers of it been assured of impunity. ("Mary, Queen of Scots," n.d.)

Such rumours could hardly have been helped by the fact that, barely three months after Darnley's murder, Mary and Bothwell were married. Bothwell had only recently obtained the divorce from Lady Jean Gordon. The marriage scandalized and divided the country, causing a number of Scotland's nobility to revolt. Catholics were particularly offended, believing the marriage to be unlawful not only on the grounds that they didn't recognize Bothwell's divorce but because the wedding had been conducted according to Protestant rites.

Things came to a head on 15 June 1567 at the Battle of Carberry Hill (a few miles east of Edinburgh), fought between supporters of Mary and the so-called Confederate Lords, a group of nobles opposed to the marriage. The Confederate Lords were intent on capturing Bothwell and putting him on trial for the murder of Darnley. On that pivotal day, Mary surrendered. The Earl of Bothwell escaped, however. He then boarded a ship and set sail with a small complement of ships, rebel forces in hot pursuit. He sailed first to the Shetland Islands and then, following a sea battle that broke the mast of one of his ships, a storm forced him to sail towards Norway, where he arrived at the port of Bergen.

The Revenge of *Skottefruen*

Although Bothwell had successfully evaded his captors by the time he arrived in Bergen, he'd managed to find himself in a textbook case of 'out of the frying pan and into the fire'. Unfortunately for poor Bothwell, but deliciously for posterity, he was detained in Bergen for lacking exit papers. Bergen, at that time, was governed by Erik Rosenkrantz – who just so happened to be the cousin of Anna Throndsen, the very same woman

Bothwell had so callously abandoned in Flanders. Throndsen had, by that time, acquired the name *Skottefruen* (the Scottish woman) from her marriage to the Scotsman. Thus, Bothwell found himself locked up in the newly built Rosenkrantz tower.

Bothwell eventually was handed over to Frederick II of Denmark. At first, the earl was treated as a welcome guest of the king. At some point, however, Bothwell had worn out his welcome and was sent to Dragsholm Castle (about 100 km from Copenhagen). Here he lived out the remaining years of his life, devoid of sanity, attached by a chain to a post, around which he slowly wore a circular groove into the floor. He died in 1578. Dragsholm Castle is rumoured to be haunted. Some say, in particular, that three ghosts linger there: a white lady, a grey lady, and James Hepburn, 4th Earl of Bothwell. Some also say that when the moon is just right, the earl can be seen riding through the courtyard in a horse and carriage ("Dragsholm Castle," n.d.).

ACT I

King of Scots

After Mary's surrender at Carberry Hill, the Confederate Lords forced her to abdicate in favour of her son, James. Thus, at 13 months old, he became James VI, King of Scots. Never to see his mother again, he was raised by governesses while Scotland was ruled by a series of four different regents until he assumed power in March 1578, just shy of his twelfth birthday.[2]

Throughout James's childhood, a power struggle ensued over who would be regent. Although there was much intrigue

---

2. The regents were: James Stewart, Earl of Moray (1567–1570); Matthew Stewart, Earl of Lennox (1570–1571); John Erskine, Earl of Mar (1571–1572); and James Douglas, Earl of Morton (1572–1581).

and violence surrounding this struggle, most of the details aren't particularly important for our purposes. He had little to no say in the decisions made by these feuding lords, although their decisions certainly affected him. What is important to note, however, is that three out of the four met violent deaths. Their fate is illustrative of how brutal sixteenth-century Scottish society was. Indeed, one of James's earliest memories was of one of these regents, his paternal grandfather, Matthew Stewart, being carried into Stirling Castle to die from his wounds in the failed coup attempt of 1571.

The Battle of Lepanto

It was also in 1571, although thousands of miles away from the petty squabbles in Scotland, that an epic naval battle was fought between the Ottoman Empire and the 'Holy League', a coalition of Catholic maritime states in the Mediterranean brought together by the Pope with the purpose of breaking Ottoman control of the eastern Mediterranean. The Holy League Fleet was comprised of ships and sailors drawn from the papal states, the Habsburg states of Spain, Naples, and Sicily, the Republic of Venice, the Republic of Genoa, the Grand Duchy of Tuscany, the Duchies of Savoy, Parma, and Urbino, and the Knights of Malta. The Supreme Commander of the fleet was John of Austria (Don Juan de Austria, in Spanish, and traditionally known as Don John of Austria, in English), the illegitimate son of Holy Roman Emperor Charles V and half-brother of Philip II of Spain.

The impetus for the formation of the Holy League was the Ottomans' ongoing attacks on the Venetian colonies on the island of Cyprus. At the time of the Holy League's formation, the Cypriot capital Nicosia had already fallen and the colony of

Famagusta was besieged. By the day of battle, all of Cyprus was in Turkish hands.

The Battle of Lepanto was fought over the course of about five hours in the Gulf of Corinth, off the coast of western Greece. It was a decisive victory for the Holy League, with over half of the Ottomans' 251 ships captured or sunk compared to the loss of only 17 League ships. Furthermore, the Holy League lost approximately the same number of men as the number of Christians they freed who were being used as enslaved oarsmen on the Ottoman galleys.

Whatever the long-term geopolitical ramifications of the victory at Lepanto, it was certainly a personal turning point for Don John of Austria, who basked in the glory as supreme commander of the victorious forces. Prior to the Battle of Lepanto, due to his status as an illegitimate son, John was denied the title of 'Your Highness', which was reserved for royals and sovereign princes. After the battle, he was addressed both in person and in letters as 'Your Highness' or 'Prince'. This honour had apparently begun to be bestowed spontaneously by his subordinates during the battle itself.

Tycho Brahe

In early November 1572, its journey of thousands of light years over, light from the Cassiopoeia supernova finally reached Earth. This event probably went unnoticed by James, who was only six years old at the time. It did not, however, escape the notice of a twenty-six-year-old Danish nobleman by the name of Tycho Brahe.

It would have been hard not to notice for a compulsive stargazer such as Tycho Brahe, since it seemed as if a new star had simply appeared out of nowhere. This 'new star' was so bright it was visible to the naked eye in the daytime. Brahe published a treatise on the matter, *De nova et nullius aevi memoria prius visa stella* (Latin for 'On the star new and never before seen in the life or memory of anyone'). 'Nova' means 'new', and it is from this treatise that the word 'supernova' derives. Eventually, the light dimmed to the point that it was no longer visible with the naked eye. The new star was a direct challenge to the Aristotelian astronomical tenet that, as opposed to the constantly changing realm of the planets, the realm of the stars was immutable.

Sporting a detachable prosthetic nose made of gold and silver, fashioned to replace the original that had been lost in a duel (allegedly over a math problem), Brahe was an astronomical genius. He was also one of the richest men in Europe at the time, and certainly the richest man in Denmark. To top it off, Brahe had been granted the island of Hven for life by Danish King Frederick II in order for him to pursue his studies of the heavens. Brahe had built a large-scale observatory, which he named Uraniborg ('The Castle of Urania'), after Urania, the ancient Greek muse of astronomy. In the observatory – which had a built-in large mural quadrant and was stocked with various other astronomical instruments, although not a telescope, which wouldn't be invented until a few years after Brahe's death – he collected detailed, accurate data on the movements of stars, which he compiled into his 'star catalogues'. He later constructed an underground facility to house those of his instruments that could be influenced by wind, naming this *Stjerneborg* ('Star Castle'), where he also put a printing press and paper mill so that all essential work could be carried out on-site. Brahe also planted an extensive set of gardens to grow various plants that he used for his other field of study: alchemy.

Tycho Brahe led a singular life. He had been kidnapped by his uncle when he was about two years old after the wee Tycho's father had reneged on a promise to give the uncle his first-born son. He had become obsessed by astronomy ever since the solar eclipse of 21 August 1560 occurred, as predicted by astronomers, when he was just thirteen. He simply overwhelmed his uncle's wish that he become a civil servant, instead pursuing astronomy with single-minded determination.

Brahe fell in love with a commoner named Kirsten, the daughter of a Lutheran minister. They were never formally married, but after three years of living together, with Kirsten wearing the keys to the household on her belt like any true wife would, they were considered husband and wife under Danish law.

One of the more bizarre anecdotes about Brahe concerns a moose that he'd been given as a gift. The moose expired after drinking too much and falling down the stairs. The moose hadn't just gotten drunk hanging around Tycho's place, by the way. Apparently, he'd had one too many beers at another nobleman's house, where he had been sent on Brahe's behalf.

It used to be thought that Brahe himself had died, in proud, early modern Danish fashion, from a burst bladder after refusing to leave the table at a piss-up (which the hard-drinking Danes apparently considered bad form). A more recent theory is that he was poisoned by his protégé, Johannes Kepler. Whether or not Kepler had anything to do with Brahe's death, he did appropriate his former mentor's star catalogues immediately afterward, which rightly belonged to Brahe's estate; Kepler used them to formulate his famous laws of planetary motion. Another theory is that Tycho was murdered by his cousin, Eric Brahe, in a hired hit put out by none other than King Christian of Denmark as vengeance for having an affair with the queen. Whatever the actual cause of his death, Tycho Brahe died as he had lived – in an interesting fashion.

An Education Fit for a King

From the age of four until the end of the regency, James was given a superlative education by a team of tutors, headed by the brilliant but abusive George Buchanan. A former tutor of the French essayist and cat fancier Michel de Montaigne, Buchanan was a humanist renowned across Europe for his Latin scholarship and poetry. He was also an accomplished playwright, writing plays in Latin. It was said that Buchanan's mastery of Latin was so great that he seemed to be writing in his native tongue.

Buchanan wrote a treatise defending the *coup d'état* orchestrated against Mary, Queen of Scots, *De Jure Regni apud Scotos* (*A Dialogue Concerning the Rights of the Crown in Scotland*), which he dedicated to wee James VI. The book was a powerful argument in favour of 'resistance theory', which had emerged from the cauldron of the Protestant Reformation. Supporters of the theory provided the moral and legal justifications for resistance to tyranny, including when and to what extent resistance was defensible. Many proponents of resistance theory, including George Buchanan, believed that tyrannicide (i.e., the killing of a tyrant for the common good) was morally justified, if not morally compulsory. Buchanan's *magnum opus* was his *Rerum Scoticarum Historia* (*History of Scotland*), published shortly before his death in 1582. Also dedicated to James, *Rerum Scoticarum Historia* is commonly cited as one of the sources for Shakespeare's *Macbeth*.

The elderly Buchanan, although ideologically a humanist, was a severe Calvinist bully to the young James. Buchanan liked to tell the young James that his mother was a villainous whore who was responsible for the death of the boy's father. Buchanan would often beat James mercilessly. After one particularly unpleasant incident of child abuse, the Countess of Mar protested, to which Buchanan replied, 'Madam, I've whipped his arse. You may kiss it if you please'. The king's terror of his former tutor never wore off completely, as he would reportedly tremble at the mere mention of his name, even as an adult.

Nevertheless, James was an eager student who responded well to the draconian curriculum. His education and learning were vast, and he ascended the throne with fluency in Scots, English, French, Latin, and Greek, as well as more than a passing familiarity with Spanish. James apparently had an impressive command of languages at an early age. A notable incident occurred when he was eight. The English ambassador was encouraged to choose a passage at random in the Bible. James was then able to translate this passage from Latin into French and then from the French into English, extemporaneously, in front of the suitably impressed ambassador.

He also gained expertise in history, law, and theology and studied military science, arithmetic, and cosmography. His education even included medicine. Together with his other studies, James was permitted to pursue his interest in the occult and the supernatural. These extracurricular subjects would remain a lifelong interest, as would a profound passion for writing and literature.

While James was enduring the harsh tutelage of Buchanan, he had another major tutor, named Peter Young, who was a much kinder and gentler director of the royal education.

Young, a respected scholar in his own right, became more of a friend and scholarly mentor to James. It was Young who was responsible for stocking and maintaining the royal library – no easy task, given the voracity of the king's reading habits.

ACT II

Esmé Stuart

In September 1579, James's dashing thirty-seven-year-old cousin, Esmé Stuart, arrived in Scotland. It was love at first sight. Their first meeting was described by one witness:

> No sooner did the young King see him, but in that hee was so neare allyed in bloud, of so renouned a Family, eminent ornaments of body and minde, tooke him up and embraced him in a most amour manner, conferred on him presently a rich inheritance; and that he might be imployed in state-affairs, elected him one of his honourable Privy Counsell, Gentleman of his Bed-chamber, and Governour of *Dumbarton* Castle. (Bergeron, 1999, p. 32)

Promotions, first to Earl of Lennox and quickly thereafter to Duke of the same, were to follow these at-first-sight honours. James was instantly infatuated with Esmé, who became the first in a series of male favourites, each a constant source of gossip and resentment among other courtiers. Esmé made an enormous impression on the thirteen-year-old boy. James wanted to be with him at all times and moped whenever they were apart for any extended period.

Whether or not Esmé immediately returned the feelings that James so publicly displayed (presumably not), there is little doubt that their relationship developed into one of mutual love and affection. Esmé even took the step of converting to Protestantism, maintaining the new faith for the rest of his life.

Esmé was instrumental in the downfall and execution of the last of the four regents, James Douglas, 4th Earl of Morton. Morton was executed on 2 June 1581 by means of the 'maiden', a proto-guillotine modelled on the Halifax gibbet. Legend has it that this particular execution was a case of poetic justice, as Morton was said to have been the one to have originally imported the 'maiden' to Scotland, having been 'impressed by its clean work' (the facts may be somewhat less poetic – it was, in fact, ordered to be built by the Edinburgh Town Council in 1564). Morton's head remained 'on the prick on the highest stone' (a spike on the north gate of the Tolbooth of Edinburgh) for eighteen months.

The Ruthven Raid

The resentment aroused by the growing power of Esmé soon resulted in an incident that's become known as the Ruthven Raid. By July 1582, a group of Protestant nobles, led by William Ruthven, 1st Earl of Gowrie, coalesced around the need to reduce the influence of French and Catholic factions in the Scottish court. The focus of this group of disgruntled nobles, who became known as the 'Lords Enterprisers', was the removal of Esmé Stuart to eliminate his hold over the young king.

On or about 22 August 1582 the conspirators struck. Having waited for the king and Esmé to be separated, and having stationed forces at a strategic location to prevent a rescue attempt by Lennox's retainers, the Lords Enterprisers seized James while he was hunting near Ruthven's castle. When, after being taken to the castle, James tried to leave the great hall and was blocked from reaching the door, he burst into tears. At this less-than-typically-Scottish display of emotion from the adolescent monarch, one of the conspirators, the Master of Glamis, was recorded as saying, 'Better bairns greet than bearded men' (better children cry than bearded men). James would never forget the remark.

Once James was securely held, the lords presented him with their 'supplication', laying out their demands and explaining the motives for their coup. This was typically Scottish – there was ample historical precedent for factions kidnapping the monarch and, in effect, holding him for 'ransom' (in exchange for policy changes, rather than money). Hence the 'supplication' – the removal/death of the monarch was never the goal in such actions, simply the ascendance of one faction of nobles over others in a traditionally rambunctious political culture. The Ruthven Raid was thus a very *Scottish* coup.

The 'Gowrie regime' ruled Scotland for about ten months, with James as a 'guest' of the Earl of Gowrie, until, in June 1583, James was able to escape his captors while on a trip to St. Andrews. Thenceforth, James was able to maintain the upper hand with his unruly nobles and begin a two-decade transformation from weak, tearful boy-king to the dominant, mature, philosopher-king fit to rule over all of the British Isles that he became. But he would never again set eyes on his beloved Esmé Stuart.

Esmé returned, in exile, to Paris, where he died shortly thereafter. Some commentators characterize this as 'dying from a broken heart'. Esmé had definitely taken the banishment hard. He had confounded the Lord's Enterprisers' expectations by remaining true to his converted faith even in the face of pressure to convert back once he was back in France. In any event, after his death, the late duke's actual heart was, pursuant to his will, packed off and sent to James. Believe it or not, this was meant as a profoundly romantic gesture, meant to symbolize that Esmé's heart really belonged not to his widow, but to his beloved James.

The Castalian Band

In the 1580s and early 1590s, James surrounded himself with a literary circle of courtiers – poets, musicians, and makars ('makar' is the Scottish equivalent of the English 'bard'). The name used to refer to this group is The Castalian Band, deriving from the 'Castalian Spring', an aquatic spring near Delphi where Roman poets were said to have gone for poetic inspiration. We know of this name from a single line by James, in an epitaph on Alexander Montgomerie: 'Quhat drowsie sleepe doth syle your eyes allace / Ye sacred brethren of Castalian band'. It is now thought unlikely that James or other 'members' of the group actually referred to themselves by this name. Nevertheless, the name is certainly a fitting shorthand for the literary circle. Artists associated with this band of brethren include the aforementioned Montgomerie, William Fowler, musician brothers Thomas and Robert Hudson, and John Stewart of Baldynneis.

In any event, the Scottish Court was the centre of a flourishing cultural scene. Experimentation and collaboration were actively encouraged. The king himself was an enthusiastic experimenter in various genres, forms, and styles of poetry. Many important translations, into Scots as well as English, were also completed in this literary environment. Again, James was active in translating. He was a particularly avid translator of his favourite poet at the time, Guillaume Salluste du Bartas, personally translating du Bartas's *L'Uranie* and commissioning Thomas Hudson to translate du Bartas's *Judit*.

William Fowler

The most noteworthy 'member' of the Castalian Band was William Fowler, whom scholar R.D.S. Jack called '[w]ithout doubt the biggest single influence in spreading a knowledge of Italian literature throughout Jacobean Scotland'. After serving as a Protestant spy in France, Fowler travelled extensively in Italy, 'which he probably visited more than once' (Jack, 1970, p. 481), enrolling at the University of Padua in 1592. He recounted in numerous poems the many places he had visited in his travels. The places that merit shout-outs in Fowler's 'Verses to Arabella Stewart', for example, include 'Lombardie, Romagnia, Mantua, Ferrara, Verona, Padua, Capua, Neapolis, Florence, Urbin, and Pavia' (Jack, 1970, p. 481). Having become fluent in Italian, Fowler was responsible for two important translations into Scottish: Petrarch's allegorical poem *Trionfi* ('Triumphs') and Machiavelli's masterpiece of political theory, *Il Principe* ('The Prince'). Fowler's translation of Machiavelli was unpublished, and it was either unfinished or possibly bowdlerized (the fact that the missing parts concerned matters that would have displeased King James gives rise to this conjecture). It was the first prose translation of a contemporary work into Scottish. In addition to his translation work, Fowler authored *The Tarantula of Love*, a Petrarchan sonnet sequence.

Du Bartas

As mentioned above, James greatly admired the French poet Guillaume de Salluste du Bartas (1544–1590). A Huguenot courtier, du Bartas spent most of his career serving at the court of Henri de Navarre (who ascended to the throne of France as Henri IV in 1589). James was able to meet his literary idol when du Bartas visited Scotland in 1587. The king attempted, unsuccessfully, to recruit du Bartas into the Castalian Band.

Essayes of a Prentise, in the Divine Art of Poesie

The young king's literary talents flourished in this artistic hothouse environment, and in 1584, he published *The Essayes of a Prentise, in the Divine Art of Poesie*. It was the first time in European history that a monarch had published his/her poetry for sale. However, as if he feared this precedent-setting status, it wasn't actually published under his name, exactly. Rather, an acrostic dedicatory poem that spelled out 'Jacobus Sextus' (Latin for 'James the 6th') playfully declared its author's identity.

The Essayes contained 'Ane Schort Treatise conteining some Reulis and Cautelis to be observit and eschewit in Scottis poesie ('A Short Treatise containing some Rules and Cautions to be observed and followed in Scottish poetry'). Herein James laid out the ground rules of his vision for a renaissance of Scottish verse. The rules were not always observed by the poets of the Castalian Band, though, including King James himself.

In fact, *The Essayes* broke a 'rule' that translation ought to be avoided as unoriginal by including a translation of du Bartas' *L'Uranie*. The inclusion of the rule discouraging translation was actually rather odd, given James's active encouragement of translation. A few notable examples of this encouragement include the king's commissioning of Thomas Hudson to translate du Bartas's *Judit,* John Stewart of Baldynneis to translate Ludovico Ariosto's highly influential *Orlando Furioso* (one of the sources for *Much Ado About Nothing*), and William Fowler to translate Petrarch and Machiavelli.

Also included in *The Essayes* was a poem entitled 'Ane Metaphoricall Invention of a Tragedie Called Phoenix'. The subject of the poem is unquestionably Esmé Stuart. Just as the acrostic dedicatory poem for the whole volume spelled out Jacobus Sextus, a preface to the Phoenix poem spells out 'Esmé Stewart Duike' on both sides of the poem; to be precise, the first letter of each line spells 'Esme Stewart Dwike', while the last letter of each line spells 'Esme Stewart Dvike'.

David Bergeron, in *King James and Letters of Homoerotic Desire*, traced the origins of the allegorical use of the phoenix (a mythical bird that dies and then rises anew from the ashes) to a locked chest full of letters written by Esmé Stuart, which he'd left behind when forced to depart Scotland. Before James was able to read them, however, 'the Advocate confessed that he had such writing and coffer, but by the commandment of Lennox he hath burnt all the writings' (Bergeron, 1999, p. 52). Bergeron identified Esmé's son as the risen phoenix:

> Out of a locked coffer of his heart James wrote *Phoenix* in response to the death of Esmé Stuart. Three actions indicate James's reaction: first, escape from his captors, which he skillfully accomplished in June 1583; second, the writing of the poem; and third, inviting Esmé's eldest son, Ludovic Stuart, to Scotland to assume his father's position and titles. This son arrived in November 1583 and remained a mainstay of the court until his death in 1624; he became the new Duke of Lennox. . . . When James wrote *Phoenix*, he constructed and offered his 'familiar letter' to and about Esmé. Through the covert allegory of the poem James voiced deep desire for his cousin, including homoerotic desire. (Bergeron, 1999, p. 53)

In her discussion of 'Phoenix', Jane Rickard wrote, 'James seems to have wanted his poem to be neither completely explicit nor entirely ambiguous'. Rickard saw in this poem the essence of one of the central tensions within James, which forms the subject of her book: 'The King's attitude toward and use of metaphor thus begins to suggest conflict between his desire to exploit poetry and his concern to control the representation and interpretation of political matters' (Rickard, 2007, p. 38).

The Essayes was printed in Edinburgh by Thomas Vautrollier. The introduction to *King James VI and I: Selected Writings* describes 'an interesting series of coincidences' that link James with

> momentous literary events in London. Thomas Vautrollier, who published James's first book of poems, *The Essayes of a Prentise*, at Edinburgh in 1584, had as his own apprentice Richard Field, a native of Stratford-upon-Avon. Vautrollier moved down to London, where he died in 1587. Field then took over the business, marrying Vautrollier's widow (or possibly his daughter), and in 1593 had the distinction of being the publisher of Shakespeare's first volume, *Venus and Adonis*. (Rhodes, Richards, & Marshall, 2003, pp. 2–3)

The Execution of Mary

After her forced abdication and subsequent flight, Mary remained imprisoned in England for over eighteen years. Elizabeth was in a difficult position. Mary was a direct threat to her crown, having at one time declared herself the true queen of England; Catholic nobles in the north of England had even mounted a rebellion in an unsuccessful attempt to replace

Elizabeth with Mary. However, she was loath to execute another sovereign monarch. She also didn't want to make Mary a Catholic martyr, as that could be even more destabilizing. Thus, Mary was kept in various great houses around England until, in 1586, she was implicated in the Babington Plot – a plan to free her and assassinate the queen. Mary was executed on 8 February 1587.

The evidence on James's personal reaction to his mother's death is conflicting. Some reports recount his sadness and indignation; others have him reacting with barely suppressed glee. As mentioned earlier, James had not set eyes upon Mary since infancy. They had exchanged letters since early childhood – a correspondence that shows James navigating a careful course of dutiful, respectful son without committing to anything that would harm either his present Scottish crown or his coveted English one. For instance, he had to diplomatically rebuff his mother's crazy request that they jointly rule Scotland. As a rule, early modern monarchs were not particularly known for their willingness to share their absolute power, not even with their own mothers (perhaps especially not with them). James was no exception. Regardless of his personal feelings, upon Mary's death, James presented a masterly performance that struck just the right balance between filial and national outrage – at the killing of his mother, an anointed queen in general, and a Scottish queen in particular – and excessive protest, so as not to jeopardize his relationship with Elizabeth.

With his mother out of the picture, James could focus on his life's greatest ambition, the English throne. From this time forward, all of his actions and decisions as King of Scotland would be made with one overriding consideration: How would it affect his chances of becoming King of England?

The Huntly Wedding Masque

In July 1588, Esmé Stuart's daughter Henrietta married George Gordon, 6th Earl of Huntly. James wrote a masque to honour the occasion. A masque was an art form unique to the early modern period. As opposed to plays, which were enjoyed by people of all classes, masques were strictly limited to noble courtiers.

Another difference between plays and masques was that, while a play was meant to be shown any number of times, a masque was a one-time event. A masque was as much a piece of political theatre as it was a work of art – meant to exalt the power of the patron. They were certainly also works of art, however: elaborate multimedia events, in fact, combining not only acting, music, singing, and poetry, but visual art and architecture as well. Indeed, the most celebrated architect of the era, Inigo Jones, was often involved in designing elaborate sets for masques. At the time, masques were the only performance art form to use scenery and sets. In contrast, if one went to see a regular play at the Globe or Blackfriars theatres, for example, the players would wear costumes and there would be the odd prop, but all of the action would be played on an empty stage.

Fragments of the masque that James wrote survive amongst his papers, although they were never published. The writing displays a mannerist aesthetic and shows off James's familiarity with *commedia dell'arte*, a form of theatre that developed in Italy in the 1550s. It uses actors wearing masks that represent archetypical, or stock, characters. Each stock character has its own standard mask and name, and sometimes a standard stance or set of mannerisms. Plays in *commedia dell'arte* were then created using these stock characters.

The masque is a dead art form, having effectively vanished in the eighteenth century. In the early twentieth century, Ralph

Vaughn Williams wrote a number of pieces that he called masques, but they aren't really comparable to those of the early modern period, being closer to ballet. Although today's typical Broadway musical would have many elements in common with a masque (e.g., acting, music, singing, spectacle), to truly replicate all of the essential components of a masque it would have to be a one-off event rather than a 'run', and the audience would have to participate. Even at that, it would still miss the central point of the masque as a display of authority and power.

Ben Jonson was a prolific writer of masques, often collaborating with Inigo Jones in creating the most celebrated and noteworthy examples of the form. There is no record of 'William Shakespeare' being involved in writing a masque. However, masque-like elements appear prominently in four Shakespeare plays: *Romeo and Juliet*, *A Midsummer Night's Dream*, *The Tempest*, and *Henry VIII*.

Anna of Denmark

In the years following his mother's death, James, now in his early twenties, began to set his sights on finding a bride. James knew that one of the best ways to make him an attractive prospect for the English throne would be to produce a good number of legitimate male heirs. Naturally, he would be all the more attractive if those heirs were the product of royalty on both sides of the family. Thus, James and his counsellors looked for prospective brides amongst the royal houses of Europe. The choices were eventually narrowed down to two candidates: Catherine, sister of Henry III of Navarre (later Henry IV of France), and Anna, the second daughter of Frederick II of Denmark. Weighing up the pros and cons, the Scots went with the Protestant option.

Anna of Denmark. Painting by Marcus Gheeraerts the Younger. Woburn Abbey, obtained from Wikimedia Commons, https://commons.wikimedia.org/wiki/File:Anne_of_Denmark_Gheeraerts.jpg

In 1589, William Fowler and an entourage were sent on a diplomatic mission to Denmark to arrange the marriage of James to Anna. Later that year, James was married to Anna 'by proxy'. Proxy marriage ceremonies, whereby ceremonies are held in each country using a 'stand-in' for the absent partner, were a common practice in early modern Europe, particularly with dynastic marriages of this sort. In the days following the conclusion of these formalities, Anna set sail for Scotland to unite with her royal groom. However, a bad storm forced the newly-wed queen's ship and all but one of the rest of the ships in the fleet to land on the shores of Norway. Upon learning of the storm, and concerned for Anna's safety, James set off from Scotland with his own fleet to retrieve his new bride. His fleet also encountered a storm that forced a stopover on the coast of Norway, where he was eventually united with his teen bride.

The newly-wed couple then travelled around Denmark for a memorable extended honeymoon. This included staying with the royal family in the newly renovated Kronborg Castle, in Helsingor. We know Helsingor, of course, as 'Elsinore'. 'James was to be based at Elsinore until early March and the pervasive mood was alcoholic', noted Alan Stewart in *The Cradle King: A Life of James VI & I*. 'The King of Scots soon acquired the habit, and Sir James Melville was only one of several who remarked on James's increasingly prodigious taste for drink. The king, Melville recorded, 'made good cheer and drank stoutly till the springtime'. In Copenhagen, he visited the Royal Academy and engaged in intellectual discourse with several learned men on a number of subjects, including theology and medicine. He remarked to the Bishop of Zealand, Povel Mathias: 'From my earliest days I have been addicted to the literary arts – and I should like to declare that today' (Stewart, 2011, p. 114).

James had a stimulating debate with Niels Hemmingsen, who'd been a student of one of Martin Luther's best mates at the University of Wittenberg. Their talk mostly revolved around predestination, a topic dear to the heart of the devoutly Calvinist Hemmingsen. James listed his meeting with Hemmingsen as one of the highlights of his trip to Denmark.

The couple reached the island of Hven on March 20 and were hosted by the island's owner, Tycho Brahe. That's right, the guy with the moose. According to *The Cradle King*: 'James had a particular interest in Brahe, because the astronomer was a correspondent of both George Buchanan and Peter Young. Brahe had sent Buchanan his treatise *De nova stella*, when he learned that Buchanan was composing a poem on the subject' (Stewart, 2011, p. 115).

The visit with Brahe made a great impression on this most intellectually curious of monarchs. He and Brahe spent a full day discussing Copernican theory (Wilson, 1959, p. 92). These ideas had been developed by Polish astronomer Nicolaus Copernicus, who published the revolutionary theory shortly before his death in 1543, in his book *De Revolutionibus orbium coelestium* (*On the Revolutions of the Heavenly Spheres*). Copernican theory adopted a heliocentric model of the cosmos (i.e., with the sun at the centre, around which all of the planets, including Earth, revolved). The unanimously accepted model of the universe since Claudius Ptolemy had been his geocentric model, wherein the sun and all of the other planets revolved around a stationary Earth.

Just as Brahe's star catalogue had finally superseded the star catalogue found in Ptolemy's *Almagest*, Copernicus's heliocentric model had been in the process of replacing Ptolemy's geocentric model in the minds of many European astronomers. Brahe was not one of these, however. He was not prepared to accept that Earth moved about the sun, although he recognized that the Copernican system was geometrically superior to the Ptolemaic one. Brahe had therefore developed his own, the 'Tychonic system', which combined the mathematical benefits of the Copernican system with the scripturally sound, and for Brahe scientifically evident, immobile Earth. The Tychonic system was a geo-heliocentric model. That is, the sun and the moon revolved around the stationary Earth, while the other planets revolved around the sun.

The Danish astronomer made such an impression on James that he was inspired to write three poems in his honour. Two of the poems refer to Brahe's 'booke', with one poem attributing almost divine powers to the 'booke'. After describing how God made mankind to rule over all of the animals of Earth, the poem suggests that God made planets to keep mankind humble towards God:

> For humble homage here before thy face (For humble homage here before your face)
> He also pitch'd eache Planet in his place (He also put each planet in its place)
> And made them rulers of the ruling Lord (And made them rulers for the ruling Lord)
> As heauenlie impes to gouerne bodies basse (As heavenly spirits to govern base bodies)
> Be subtle and celestiall sweete accord (By subtle and celestial sweet accord)
> Then greate is Ticho who by this his booke (Then great is Tycho who by this his book)
> Commandement doth ouer these commanders brooke.
> (Allows commandment over these commanders.)

The 'booke' to which James refers in the first two sonnets is Brahe's star catalogue. A star catalogue is essentially a list of stars with observed data, such as its position in the sky. Not published until almost a decade after James's visit to Hven, Brahe's was the first star catalogue to fully supersede Ptolemy's second-century astronomical masterpiece, the *Almagest*. It was also the last to be produced without the aid of the telescope. The development of the refracting telescope would not occur until 1608 (initially in The Netherlands, with improvements by Galileo shortly thereafter), seven years after the Dane's death.

Unfortunately, history does not record whether James met Tycho's moose.

English Players in Scotland

When the newlywed couple arrived in Scotland after their extended honeymoon, there were further festivities as the Scots had their turn to celebrate the marriage. Queen Elizabeth sent an acting company to add to the entertainment.

James developed an ongoing relationship with this acting company, inviting them to Scotland at least four times, in 1589, 1594, 1599, and 1601. The only name attached to these otherwise anonymous players is a shadowy figure by the name of Laurence (or Lawrence) Fletcher. Fletcher's Wikipedia article calls him a 'man of mystery':

> He is listed on the royal patent of 19 May 1603 that transformed the Lord Chamberlain's Men into the King's Men – and he is listed first, with William Shakespeare second and Richard Burbage third; significant in the hierarchy-mad world of the time. Yet Fletcher never appears on the other

documents that give later generations our limited knowledge of the King's Men; he doesn't seem to have acted, in the leading company of the age. ("Lawrence Fletcher," n.d.)

James was delighted by the travelling players and very protective of them while they were in Scotland. He had to be. Plays were usually banned there, and players had the same sort of unsavoury reputation for licentiousness and disorderliness that they had in England. Unlike in London, where plays were also banned but the theatres and acting companies had been able to set up shop outside of the city limits, there was no such loophole in Scotland. The Scottish Church, or Kirk, as it was called, took a particularly dim view of these players being allowed into their midst. When some ministers took to preaching in their sermons against the players' presence in Edinburgh, James instructed the ministers to tell their congregations at their next sermon that they had been very much mistaken, and that of course the visiting players were welcome guests in Scotland.

Jenny Wormald described the king's relationship with the English players:

> English actors, comedians, seem to have been invited again in 1594, presumably for the baptism of his first son, Henry. Certainly Laurence Fletcher was known to the King by this time and Fletcher and his men were back in 1599 causing a furious row between James and the Edinburgh clergy, which the King won. They may indeed have stayed on in Scotland for the tour that begun in 1601, when they went on tour to Dundee and Aberdeen and Fletcher's name heads the list, with Shakespeare second, on the letters of patent to the King's Men in May, 1603. (Wormald, 2000, p. 253)

The Honeymoon Ends

Although the first few years of marriage with Anne seemed loving enough, the couple soon fought over how to raise their first son, Henry. James insisted that he be sent away to live, as he himself had done as a boy, with the Earl of Mar and his family. Anna naturally wanted her child to live with her and found the thought of being separated from Henry almost unbearable. James, however, knew only too well Scottish royalty's vulnerability in Scotland's rowdy political culture. They would all be safer if the king was kept separate from his heir apparent (much like the U.S. vice-president is kept separate from the president). He wouldn't budge on the matter, and Henry lived separately from the rest of the royal family until they all moved to London in 1603.

For most of the rest of their marriage, they seldom spoke, although there were times of at least the appearance of genuine affection. In any event, James did not hold a particularly high opinion of women and preferred the company of men, both inside and outside of the bedchamber. Nevertheless, the couple produced three children who survived infancy: two sons, Henry (born 1594) and Charles (born 1600), and a daughter, Elizabeth, (born 1596).

The North Berwick Witch Trials

On All Hallows Eve of 1589, in St. Andrew's Auld Kirk Green in North Berwick, Scotland, upwards of 200 hundred townsfolk gathered for a meeting of the most diabolical nature. The townsfolk, all witches, had come to make a pact with the devil. In exchange for bestowing a multitude of worldly powers on each witch, the devil's side of the bargain had only one term: the witches were to use their occult powers to attempt to kill the devil's single greatest enemy on Earth, James VI, King of Scots. The parties consummated the pact with an orgy during which the Prince of Darkness enjoyed repeated bouts of anilingus. That was how King James told it, at any rate.

If you won't take his word for it, consider the word of one Agnes Sampson, who confessed to the whole sordid, satanic conspiracy. Whether or not you take her word for it depends upon the extent to which you think her story should be discounted by the fact that it was arrived at after she had been stripped naked, shorn of all body hair, tortured, and then kept awake for days on end in an early modern torture device known as a 'witch's bridle'. The particular witch's bridle used on Sampson was made of iron and had four sharp prongs – two pressed against the tongue and two pressed against the cheeks. The bridle was then fastened to the wall. Prior to being tortured, Sampson had steadfastly denied being a witch or having anything to do with the devil. King James, if you take him at his word, had believed her denials right up until she was able to repeat to him the very words that had passed between James and his bride on their wedding night in Oslo.

Returning to the events of All Hallows Eve in North Berwick, the devil made it clear to all those assembled at the Black Sabbath that the man he fancied to replace James as King of Scots was Francis Stewart, 5th Earl of Bothwell. This Earl of Bothwell was the nephew of the 4th Earl of Bothwell (remember him? – he was the third and final husband of Mary, Queen of Scots), and a cousin of King James. Francis Stewart had obtained the title of Earl of Bothwell at a ceremony in Stirling Castle in 1577. Although James Hepburn, 4th Earl of Bothwell, was still technically alive in 1577, at that point he was stark raving mad, tied to a post in a Danish prison, and neither hide nor hair had been seen of him in Scotland since he'd fled the field of battle at Carberry Hill. Although Francis Stewart, 5th of Earl of Bothwell, had once been a favourite of James, by the end of the 1580s he had become, according to David H. Wilson, the man 'whom the King feared and hated above all other living men' (Wilson, 1959, p. 100).

The king's version had the advantage of explaining all of the terrible weather that had surrounded his marriage to Anna. You see, the witches had caused the initial storms that had forced Anna's ships back to the coast of Norway. They knew that James, man of honour that he was, would have no choice but to set sail to rescue her. They would then have him just where they wanted: vulnerable in the open ocean. It would then be a simple matter of raising another storm and sinking his boat, thus drowning the devil's mortal enemy once and for all. This would also give them two shots at the King – one on the way from Scotland to Denmark and another on the way back. They very nearly succeeded, too. Terrible storms threatened the royal couple all of the way from Denmark to Scotland, and the King's ship almost capsized as it neared the Scottish coast. If you think about it, the foul weather *must* have been the work of witches fulfilling the terms of a demonic pact. How else would you explain storms in the North Sea in November?

It is said that the bald, naked, mutilated ghost of Agnes Sampson roams Holyrood Palace, haunting James's descendants to this very day. This hardly seems unreasonable, given the circumstances.

His Maiesties Poeticall Exercises at Vacant Houres

In 1591, James published *His Maiesties Poeticall Exercises at Vacant Houres*. Other than a few sonnets that he later added to some of his prose works, it would be the last poetry that James published until 1618.

Included in this volume of poetry is 'Lepanto', an epic narrative poem recounting the events of the Battle of Lepanto. 'Lepanto' was republished upon James's accession to the throne. The poem imagines the victory of Christian Europe ('the baptiz'd race') over the Ottomans ('circumcised Turban Turkes') as the result of divine intervention, since God, weighing up the sins of both sides, found:

> The Christian faults with faithless Turkes,
> The balance stood not eaven,
> But sweid upon the faithless side

So, God sends the Archangel Gabriel to Venice to 'put into their minds to take revenge of wrongs the Turks have done in sundrie kinds'. Here's how the young monarch describes Venice (capitalization of MARKE in the original):

> This Towne it stands with the Sea,
> Five miles or there about,
> Upon no Ile nor ground, the Sea
> Runnes all the streets throughout.
> Who stood upon the Steeple head
> Should see a wondrous sight,
> A Towne to stand without a ground,
> Her ground is made by slight:
> Strong Timber props dung in the Sea
> Do beare her up by art,
> An Ile is all her market place
> A large and spacious part,

> A Duke with Senate joynd doth rule,
> Saint MARKE is patron cheife,
> Ilk yeare they wedde the Sea with rings
> To be their sure reliefe. (Rhodes, Richards, & Marshall, 2003, p. 100)

The poem then describes how the Christian nations coalesced, sending troops and ships that assembled into a force at Messina, Sicily. The force leaves Messina under the command of Don John of Austria (whom James refers to in the poem as Don Joan), and then the Battle of Lepanto is described in grand detail. Despite the depiction of Don John in a heroic light, James inserted a preface to the reader that referred to the victorious commander as 'a foreign Papist bastard' and blamed readers for misunderstanding his intentions if they thought he was exalting Don John in particular. He explained that he had not intended to give Don John credit for the victory, that 'what so ever praise I have given to DON-JOAN in this Poem, it is neither in accompting him as first or second cause of that victory, but only as of a particular man', since it wouldn't become his honour as a monarch 'like a hireling, to pen the praise of any man' (Rhodes, Richards, & Marshall, 2003, pp. 94–95).

Also included in *Poeticall Exercises* was another translation of a poem by Guillaume de Salluste Du Bartas – this time 'Les Furies'. Du Bartas reciprocated with a French translation of 'Lepanto', which was included in *Poeticall Exercises* along with James's English version.

The Succession Question

Elizabeth I was fifty-three when she executed Mary, Queen of Scots. One thing had been certain for some time: Elizabeth, the Virgin Queen, would not be succeeded by a child of her own.

Exactly who would succeed the ageing queen was anything but certain. This uncertainty was problematic. For the monarchies of early modern Europe, the question of succession was paramount. Political stability was dependent upon consensus over who should get to wear the crown – at least, consensus among those powerful enough to field or finance an army. As we have already seen, England in the previous century had descended into over thirty years of civil war after this consensus of the powerful had broken down.

The execution of Mary had induced Philip II of Spain to attempt an invasion of England. After this immediate existential threat had been neutralized by England's defeat of the Spanish Armada in 1588, the question of the succession again occupied the minds of Elizabeth's subjects. It was only natural; the identity of the next monarch would have great consequences, particularly when it came to the delicate issue of religion. A contested succession could be disastrous.

Yet Elizabeth had, since 1581, expressly forbidden anyone to openly discuss the matter, upon pain of death. The simple reason was that, while it may have been in the interest of everyone who would live in the wake of Elizabeth's death to have the succession question settled, such certainty was contrary to Elizabeth's interests. She knew full well that if she named a successor, power would instantly flow out of her hands and into those of the nominee, as courtiers sought influence and favour with the monarch of tomorrow rather than the elderly queen. Why accept present instability for future stability? Why make somebody else's problem her own? Elizabeth was nobody's fool. Not taking any chances, she had parliament pass the *Act against Seditious Words and Rumours Uttered against the Queen's Most Excellent Majesty*, which made it a capital offence to publish speculation on the succession.

In light of this ban, the discussion was carried on privately and secretly, often by the clandestine exchange of unpublished manuscripts. It was also carried on publicly, however, through a very active trade in treatises on the subject, which were generally published anonymously, pseudonymously, or by foreigners living safely outside of England. These treatises are known as 'succession tracts'.

It is easy to get bogged down by the minutiae of claims to the throne. The main thing was to show direct descent from a previous legitimate monarch, of course, but many legal considerations could be applied. One of the main ones, which we typically take for granted, is primogeniture. Remember the Wikipedia definition of primogeniture:

> In primogeniture (or more precisely *male primogeniture*) the monarch's eldest son and his descendants take precedence over his siblings and their descendants. Elder sons take precedence over younger sons, but all sons take precedence over all daughters. Children represent their deceased ancestors, and the senior line of descent always takes precedence over the junior line, within each gender. The right of succession belongs to the eldest son of the reigning monarch, and then to the eldest son.

Primogeniture was the cornerstone of James's claim to the English throne. There were no surviving descendants of Elizabeth or of her father, Henry VIII, and the male line from Henry VII had ended with the death of Edward VI, in 1553. Accordingly, following primogeniture, the right of succession would fall to direct descendants of Margaret Tudor, Henry VII's eldest daughter. Margaret was James's great-grandmother; she had married James IV of Scotland, subsequently giving birth to

James's grandfather, James V. James V was the father of Mary, Queen of Scots. Strictly following the rules of primogeniture, James was, after his mother's death, next in line to the throne of England.

But there were a number of impediments to a straightforward claim based strictly on primogeniture. The succession tract genre was essentially concerned with arguing for or against the application of some or all of these impediments. Some succession tracts supported or opposed a particular claimant, while others weighed up the pros and cons of a range of candidates, more or less fairly. While all of the tracts were partisan to some extent, sometimes the bias was blatant, but at other times the writer appears to have been at least attempting objectivity. Religion was often a driving motivation – for example, in tracts arguing for or against Catholic claimants. More often than not, it's fair to describe any given succession tract as quite clearly either pro-James or anti-James.

There were four main impediments to James's claim:

1. his foreign birth;
2. the *Act of Association*;
3. certain provisions of Henry VIII's will;
4. Henry VII's descent from a junior line of the House of Lancaster.

Some tracts invoked an archaic statute, *De natis ultra mare*, from 1351, that restricted inheritance by foreign-born children. This argument is mercifully straightforward – James's foreign birth in Scotland, rather than England, disqualified his claim. Were this impediment to be operative, and James disqualified, primogeniture would favour his cousin, Arabella Stuart. Like James, Arabella's great-grandmother was Margaret Tudor. Unlike James, Arabella had been born and raised in England.

Another potential obstacle was the *Act of Association*, passed in 1585. This statute excluded from the English succession the heirs of anyone found guilty of seeking the death of Queen Elizabeth. Mary, Queen of Scots, had been found guilty of this very thing. However, this statute was ultimately ignored.

Henry VIII, through parliament's passage of the *Third Succession Act*, had been granted the right to dispose of the English crown in his will (irrespective of the rules of primogeniture). His will included a provision expressly meant to exclude his Scottish relatives from inheriting the crown in the event that his legitimate children (at the time, this included his only son, Edward, and two daughters, Elizabeth and Mary) did not continue the line of succession. The will stated that in this case, succession should proceed through his younger sister, Mary Tudor, and not through his elder sister, Margaret Tudor. If Henry's will had been followed at the time of Elizabeth's death, a woman named Anne Stanley, Countess of Castlehaven, would have become queen. If Henry's will had been followed and Elizabeth had died before 1596, Anne Stanley's grandmother, Margaret Stanley, Countess of Derby would have become queen (she died in 1596, after her son, Anne's father).

The fourth and final main impediment to James's claim, one that downgraded descent from Henry VII, was rather complicated. Proponents argued that the rules of primogeniture actually entailed going farther back than Henry VII. Confusingly, it argued that descent should be traced to someone who had never even been King of England: John of Gaunt, Duke of Lancaster. John of Gaunt, you will recall, was the father of Henry IV. The argument boils down to the fact that Henry VII traced his descent, and therefore his claim to the throne, from a younger daughter of John of Gaunt. Claimants who could trace a line of descent from John of Gaunt's eldest daughter, it was asserted, actually conformed better to the dictates of primogeniture, since 'the senior line of descent always takes precedence over the junior line, within each gender'. This argument was generally favoured by those who supported a Catholic claimant, since this eldest daughter had married into the Portuguese House of Aviz. Notice that this line of reasoning essentially treats the entire Tudor dynasty as if it had never happened.

There was even an argument, made earlier in Elizabeth's reign, that supported a Yorkist claim by declaring Henry VII a usurper (i.e., asserting he had wrongfully taken the throne from the rightful king, Richard III). Unsurprisingly, this view gained no traction.

It's important to realize that the successful claimant would not be determined solely (or even primarily) by who could make the most persuasive legal argument. Rather, he or she would need to demonstrate support, primarily amongst members of the nobility and the landed gentry. When it came to attracting support – irrespective of the law or the rules of primogeniture – each claimant, including James, had natural advantages and disadvantages that played to or against an Englishman's prejudices. With all else being equal, for example, a man would be favoured over a woman. James, as a Scot, was less desirable than an Englishman, but he had an obvious advantage over a Spaniard (since England was at war with Spain).

Catholic claimants attracted Catholic support; Protestants attracted Protestant support. An interesting consequence of this was that the execution of Mary, Queen of Scots, caused each side to swap their arguments: those that Catholics had used to support Mary's succession were dropped by them and taken up by Protestants, and vice versa. Protestant support was, obviously, more important in late sixteenth-century England than Catholic support.

James had a number of other qualities that made him an attractive claimant. First and foremost, he had work experience as a monarch. As the 1590s progressed, he had an ever-expanding CV of successful rule in Scotland. It was one thing to be Countess of Castlehaven, quite another to rule over a whole country. James had demonstrated that he could rule.

Another increasingly appealing factor was the presence of offspring. Prince Henry had been born in 1594. By the time Anna gave birth to Charles, a back-up male heir, in 1600, Henry was a hearty and healthy six-year-old with a four-year-old sister, Elizabeth. Large families were insurance policies for stability. The more potential heirs that a claimant could show, the more attractive s/he became, since they reduced the chances of the country having to go through another tense period of uncertain succession.

One of the most important succession tracts was published in 1594, under the pseudonym of 'R. Doleman'. The Doleman tract, as it is known, reignited the succession debate and spawned a number of tracts in response. Universally believed to have been written by the Jesuit Robert Persons (perhaps with others), the Doleman tract considered the respective merits of fourteen different claimants, although its main purpose appears to have been to argue the case against James. It was widely assumed at the time to favour the claim of the Spanish Infanta, Isabella Clara Eugenia. What is certain is that it took a Catholic perspective. The Doleman tract argued against primogeniture, supported resistance theory, and proposed elective, rather than hereditary, monarchy. James took the publication extremely seriously.

This is how D.H. Wilson has described the Doleman tract:

[The tract's author] examined with a clever pretence at impartiality the claims and qualifications of all possible heirs to the English throne. But he found objections to every candidate, and to James in particular, until he came to consider the absurd pretensions of Philip of Spain and of his daughter, the Infanta Isabella Clara Eugenia, descendants of John of Gaunt. In Parson's skilful hands, the claims of Philip and the Infanta became impeccable and the object of the book grew clear. It was Spanish propaganda and very effective. At James it was a double thrust; it denied the principle of hereditary right and disabled his personal qualifications, leaving him outraged and aghast. (Wilson, 1959, p. 140)

Wilson went on to describe the King's reaction to this 'double thrust':

Terrified lest the great prize slip away, he embarked upon many activities of which one was literary. In both the *Trew Lawe* and the *Basilikon Doron* he answered Parsons by stressing the hereditary nature of kingship. Hereditary right, he asserted, was God's method of selecting kings; the right of the lawful heir was inalienable and indefeasible; and to him the people were bound as fully as to the ruling sovereign. They could no more reject the one than depose the other. The throne was never vacant, 'for at the very moment of the expiring of the king reigning, the nearest and lawful heir entereth in his place'. This – James's great argument – he repeated over and over again. (Wilson, 1959, pp. 140–141)

James seems to have regarded his cousin Arabella Stuart as his biggest rival. Although James could generally be relied upon to show leniency and mercy, in Arabella's case, he displayed an excessive abundance of caution that veered into cruelty. A decade into James's English reign, she starved herself to death in the Tower of London after James had mercilessly imprisoned her for marrying without his permission.

James adjusted his policies in running Scotland when he thought doing so would help his claim. One Jesuit wrote that King James would accept the English crown from the Devil himself. Throughout the 1590s, James proved an able ruler in Scotland, consolidating his power over both the nobility and the Kirk, all the while negotiating, manoeuvring, and grovelling with his cousin Elizabeth both with respect to an annual stipend she provided and in an attempt to become her named successor. The farthest she would go, however, was to agree not to prejudice his claim.

The Faerie Queene

The Faerie Queene is an unfinished epic poem written by the English writer Edmund Spenser. Set during the time of Arthurian legend, it is an elaborate allegory in which the characters represent abstract virtues/vices but also allude to real people of the age. For instance, the central character of Gloriana, the Faerie Queene of the title, represents the abstract virtue of glory but is also an unmistakeable allusion to Queen Elizabeth, to whom the poem was dedicated. The shameless sucking up paid off, with Spenser receiving an annual pension of fifty pounds from the queen. A massive project, Spenser published the poem in instalments of three 'parts' each, of which he originally intended at least twelve. The first instalment – that is, Parts I through III – appeared in 1590. The next instalment, Parts IV through VI, which turned out to be the last Spenser published before his death, was released in 1596.

Part V happened to include a character named Duessa, the daughter of Deceit and Shame, who represented falsity. The fact that Duessa was also a clear allusion to Mary, Queen of Scots, infuriated James – at least, he sure made a bloody good show of anger to the English ambassador. The book was immediately banned in Scotland, and the king called for Spenser's arrest and punishment for insulting not only 'his mother deceased' but James himself.

Giacomo Castelvetro

Giacomo Castelvetro was an Italian Protestant writer best known today for *The Fruit, Herbs, and Vegetables of Italy*; he wrote this after being shocked and appalled by the English diet, which he saw as far too heavy in meat and far too light in fresh, green vegetables. Castelvetro would no doubt have concurred with Sir Andrew Aguecheek's self-assessment in *Twelfth Night*: 'I am a great eater of beef and I believe that does harm to my wit'. Castelvetro had fled religious persecution in his native Modena as a young man and travelled around Europe for many years, including extended periods in Vienna and Basel, before settling for a time in England. There he received the patronage of poet-courtier Philip Sidney as well as Elizabeth I's infamous spymaster, Sir Francis Walsingham.

In 1592, James hired Castelvetro as tutor of Italian to both James and Queen Anna. He would teach the royal couple for three years. In typical Jacobean fashion, the studies were highly effective, and by 1595, James could add Italian to the already impressive list of languages in which he was fluent.

Incidentally, James was able to rescue Castelvetro from execution by the Inquisition in Venice in 1611 by having his ambassador threaten a diplomatic incident if the execution were carried out. Castelvetro managed to escape 'the furious bite of the cruel and pitiless Roman inquisition' and made his way back to England. His brother, less fortunate, was burned at the stake.

The Octavians

One of James's greatest challenges as a monarch was in the area of finances. He was constantly in debt, so his counsellors were forever devising ways to wring more money out of his subjects. It wasn't that James himself led a particularly ostentatious lifestyle. He often dressed more plainly than many of his courtiers, for example. But he was constantly bestowing gifts and honours at a rate that outpaced his income. He had a very difficult time refusing requests. Ever the wily politician, James also used patronage and other rewards to manipulate subjects for his purposes.

Whatever the causes, James was generally mindful that the continual financial difficulties presented a challenge to the effectiveness and prestige of his monarchy. Sometimes his acute awareness of this fact led to moments of clarity. One such instance was precipitated when Queen Anna presented him with a sack of gold coins as a New Year's present for 1596. Surprised by his wife's superior ability to have a sack of gold available while he had his usual nuppence, he asked her how she'd managed such a feat. Anna explained that a group of her advisors had been able to help her save money by making economies. Suitably impressed, James decided to hire those advisors as his own financial gurus.

The committee of eight, known as the 'Octavians', met with some initial success in straightening out the royal finances. However, the imposition of new taxes together with a tightening of purse strings attracted the ire of a diverse range of subjects. The resultant unpopularity ultimately led to a riot in Edinburgh. This turmoil, together with the king's inability to stick with any long-term reform of his spending habits, led to the disbanding of the committee by the year's end.

Daemonologie

James first published his treatise on witches and witchcraft, *Daemonologie*, in 1597. It was republished in 1603 upon his accession to the English throne. The book is written in the form of a dialogue between two characters, Philomathes and Epistemon. Its three parts deal with (1) magic in general, (2) sorcery and witchcraft, and (3) the spirits and spectres that appear and trouble people. The last third of the treatise also contains an account of the North Berwick Witch Trials, naturally painting a very flattering picture of the king's role in the trial. The stated aim of *Daemonologie* is to prove the existence of all of these various 'devilish arts' and to delineate what severe punishment they deserve. The introduction to *King James VI and I: Collected Writings* contains the following passage, remarkable for demonstrating a straight line from *Daemonologie* to the plot of *Hamlet*:

> Some of the most interesting parts of *Daemonologie* are those which deal with borderline areas, raising knotty issues that Epistemon takes it upon himself to resolve. He warns Philomathes that evil spirits may just as easily take the form of a virtuous person as a wicked one, and explains (as Hamlet feared) how the devil may appear in the likeness of someone recently deceased to tell how they were murdered (II, i–ii). Towards the end of the dialogue he also raises the matter of fairy belief and describes how some witches talk of being

transported to a hill that opened to reveal the Fairy Queen and her court. (Rhodes, Richards, & Marshall, 2003, p. 11)

The True Law of Free Monarchies

James entered the ongoing succession tract fray personally with the 1598 publication of *The True Law of Free Monarchies; or The Reciprocal and Mutual Duty Betwixt a Free King and His Natural Subjects*. Once again publishing under a pseudonym, he signed the preface 'Philopatris', Greek for 'lover of one's country', but it was an open secret that James was the author.

A fairly straightforward treatise on the nature of monarchy, it set out for general consumption the king's thoughts on the matter. Don't let the full title fool you – by 'reciprocal and mutual duty', James meant that it was a king's duty to tell everyone what to do, and it was everyone else's duty to bloody well do whatever the king commanded.

The cornerstone of the treatise was the doctrine of the divine right of kings. Essentially, proponents of divine right argued that a monarch's right to rule was derived from the will of God himself; monarchs therefore were answerable only to God and not subject to any earthly power whatsoever. The divine right of kings, although its origins lay in medieval thinking about church and state, was a political theory that had arisen from the Protestant Reformation, as Protestant princes sought to limit any sort of radical notion that they could be held accountable for their sins. James was a leading proponent of divine right theory.

Correlatively, *True Law* was an attack on resistance theory. As we have seen earlier, James's childhood tutor, George Buchanan, had been a major proponent of this view, which held that it was morally justified, if not morally compulsory, to resist tyrants.

James drew on references to the Old Testament Hebrew kings, praising 'the forme of gouernement established among them, especially in a Monarchie[, which,] . . . as resembling the Diuinitie, approacheth nearest to perfection, as all the learned and wise men from the beginning haue agreed vpon'.

Basilikon Doron

James composed *Basilikon Doron* (Greek for 'Royal Gift') for his eldest son and heir apparent, Prince Henry. It was written in the form of a private letter addressed to Henry, and he presented it as a gift to the five-year-old lad in 1599. A common practice of early modern monarchs, such works were summations of advice on kingship and ruling, like instruction manuals that royal fathers gave to their sons. *Basilikon Doron* was originally meant to be circulated to the prince and a small group of courtiers. In fact, although only seven copies were originally printed, it ended up being published and then became a bestseller when republished in 1603, upon his ascension to the English throne.

Basilikon Doron starts with a sonnet that simply assumes the divine right of kings:

> GOD giues not Kings the stile of Gods in vaine,
> For on his Throne his Scepter doe they swey:
> And as their subjects ought them to obey,
> So Kings should feare and serue their God againe
> If then ye would enjoy a happie raigne,
> Obserue the Statutes of your heauenly King,
> And from his Law, make all your Lawes to spring:
> Since his Lieutenant here ye should remain,
> Reward the iust, be stedfast, true, and plaine,

Represse the proud, maintayning aye the right,
Walke alwayes so, as euer in his sight,
Who guardes the godly, plaguing the prophane:
And so ye shall in Princely vertues shine,
Resembling right your mightie King Diuine.

James may have modelled *Basilikon Doron* on Holy Roman Emperor Charles V's *Political Testament,* addressed to the emperor's son Philip. Giacomo Castelvetro had given the king an Italian version of *Political Testament* in 1592 (Peck, 1991, p. 47).

The Gowrie Plot

The events of 5 August 1600 have come to be variously known as the Gowrie Plot, the Gowrie Conspiracy, or the Gowrie Mystery. Depending upon where you place the preponderance of evidence, James either miraculously escaped almost certain death by the skin of his teeth *or* he cold-bloodedly directed the murder of a pair of brethren, then covered it up with the power of the state and what might charitably be called a likely story.

The king's story went as follows: He and some buddies were out hunting near Falkland Palace on the fateful day, when they were approached by Alexander Ruthven, the younger brother of John Ruthven, 3rd Earl of Gowrie. Ruthven told them that he'd witnessed some sort of shady character, possibly a papal agent or perhaps even a Jesuit spy, burying a pot of gold in a field outside of Perth! Although the King was, as he was careful to note, at first highly doubtful of this outlandish claim (James was nobody's fool, after all), young Ruthven was somehow able to convince the otherwise most wily and cautious monarch to follow him back to Gowrie House, where his brother held the man captive so that James might interrogate him.

James arrived at Gowrie House with a small number of retainers. After dinner there, according to the official story, James was induced to follow Alexander Ruthven upstairs, alone. Here, the facts seem to be most hazy in any account of the story. At some point, the King perceived that his life was in danger and was able to shout to his guardsmen. After the dust settled, both Alexander and his brother John were dead. There were no other fatalities.

The king took steps to ensure that his subjects didn't enquire too deeply into the story. Church ministers were ordered by the Crown to give thanks in their sermons for the king's deliverance; those who failed to obey were imprisoned and/or removed from office. Just to make sure that everyone understood exactly how subjects were supposed to feel about this turn of events – namely, jubilant that their beloved king had safely prevailed over this most wicked treachery – James declared 5 August to be a national holiday thenceforth.

It must be noted that the Earl of Gowrie, at the time of his death, was by far the Crown's largest creditor. How fortuitous for James that one day's events could avenge the treachery that had driven his first love from him *and* release him from a most inconvenient debt. Some historians tend to buy the king's story. Personally, I fall squarely into the 'pull the other one, Your Majesty, it's got bells on it' camp.

ACT III

The Essex Rebellion

By the turn of the century, Elizabeth was in her late sixties and had been on the throne for over forty years. One of the consequences of this long reign was that a great number of her subjects either had never experienced or could barely remember life under a different monarch. The tumultuous years between Henry VIII's death and Elizabeth's accession, in the late 1540s and 1550s, was a distant memory, and then for only the oldest. However, the shine was gradually wearing off Gloriana as she entered her dotage.

Since the high point of the glorious defeat of the Spanish Armada, England seemed to be in decline. The economy, increasingly strained by the costs associated with the ongoing conflict with Spain as well as the Nine Years' War with Ireland (1595–1603),[3] had been hit with a series of poor harvests. Prices consequently rose, the standard of living declined for most of Elizabeth's subjects, and inequality continued to grow; indeed, the parallels, in macro-economic terms, between early seventeenth-century Britain and early twenty-first-century Britain are striking. Consequently, Elizabeth faced escalating criticism over the course of the 1590s.

The turn of the century also found James at the peak of his impatience to seize control of the much richer and more powerful kingdom to his south. Furthermore, he was becoming increasingly concerned that, while England and Spain were still officially at war, hostilities were cooling. It had been over a decade since the Armada's defeat, and alarming signs of peace had begun to appear, such as the tentative (although ultimately abortive) negotiations held in early 1600. While he could usually be counted on to support peace, James knew that his royal claim was safer if England was at war with Spain, and he started to get nervous. He began to contemplate desperate measures, including the possibility of raising an army to claim

---

3. Also known as Tyrone's Rebellion, the Nine Years' War was an unsuccessful attempt by a number of Irish chieftains and their allies to limit the expansion of English state power in Ireland.

the throne by force. The insanity of such an idea was not lost on his Scottish subjects – a body called 'the convention of estates' refused to approve a tax on raising such an army, and James decided not to press the issue (Lee, 1990, p. 101).

The 1590s had also seen changes in the English Privy Council, the monarch's closest political advisors, analogous to a cabinet of ministers. A number of important members had died in the late 1580s and early 1590s, creating a less stable Privy Council – one more susceptible to factional rivalry. One of the more consequential rivalries arose between Robert Cecil, the son of William Cecil (Lord Burghley), and Robert Devereux, the Earl of Essex. The temperaments of the two men couldn't have been more different. Robert Cecil, the Lord High Treasurer's hunchbacked second son, was similar to his father – intelligent, wily, deliberate, cautious, and loyal – all qualities that would later form the basis for mutually beneficial service under James. The Earl of Essex, on the other hand, was dashing, combative, impetuous, impulsive, and rebellious. Essex enjoyed wide popularity in London and was perceived as a champion of Protestantism. By the turn of the century, the Privy Council was divided between these two sides, with the Cecil faction emerging as the more dominant.

One of the most important issues upon which the two factions differed was in choosing a successor for Elizabeth. In order to understand this distinction, however, it is important to understand that Elizabeth had steadfastly refused to name a successor for the eminently prudent reason that doing so would immediately put her life in danger. The older Elizabeth got, the more paranoid she became with respect to the destabilizing effects of the succession issue.

Essex clearly favoured James. Indeed, he had declared in writing his support for the Scottish king's succession. James relied on Essex to be his spokesman at the Elizabethan court, starting around 1598. But there was a mutual mistrust between James and Robert Cecil. James, who had never liked Robert's father, correctly perceived the younger Cecil as being more open to compromise with Spain. James was less correct in falling for Essex's wilder, self-serving claims regarding the Cecil faction's desire for a Spanish successor to the English throne. In any event, James – quite secretly and definitely unofficially – cast his lot with the Essex faction.

By 1599, Essex had already proven himself to be particularly insubordinate to Queen Elizabeth. In 1589, he had defied her order to not take part in the unsuccessful Counter Armada, led by Francis Drake after the defeat of the Spanish Armada. While this earlier incident might have been chalked up to a youthful giddiness to 'get out into the shit', so to speak, Essex displayed a much more dangerous lack of judgement during his command of a 1597 naval expedition known as the Islands Voyage. Tasked with neutralizing a Spanish battle fleet near the Azores, with a secondary objective of capturing her treasure fleet, Essex disobeyed Elizabeth by pursuing the treasure fleet first. The expedition ended up failing in all of its objectives, including those respecting the treasure fleet, at the cost of many English casualties.

Despite his record of imprudence and disobedience, Elizabeth appointed Essex Lord Lieutenant of Ireland, in 1599, in the midst of the Nine Years' War. Commanding the largest army to take to the field during Elizabeth's reign (16,000 men), Essex was widely expected to put a quick and decisive end to the conflict. Instead, he ended up agreeing to a truce with a rebel leader. After racing back to England in order to give Elizabeth his version of events before the Cecil faction could put their spin on it, he burst in on the queen in the midst of her daily dressing and makeup application ordeal. A furious Elizabeth called his conduct as Lord Lieutenant 'perilous and contemptible'. The truce was seen as an unforgivable humiliation for mighty England. He was stripped of his offices and placed under house arrest. A few months later, particularly after Elizabeth began to perceive some advantage to the truce, Essex was allowed his freedom. However, the Queen refused to restore his monopoly on sweet wine. For the already financially pressed Essex, this created both great resentment and desperation. Thus were sown the seeds of his attempted *coup d'état*.

On 3 February 1601, five of the principal conspirators to this plot met at a house in London owned by the Earl of Southampton, to finalize plans; Essex, to avoid arousing suspicion, was not present. The conspirators agreed to a plan: on the day in question, they would attempt to rouse the population of London by claiming that Cecil's faction had hijacked the government and were planning on murdering Essex and selling out England to the Spanish. With the support of the people, the rebels would then convince the queen to accept three main demands: that she remove Robert Cecil and his faction from court, grant them a private audience (at which she would be obliged to name James as her successor), and call a session of parliament. Note that the plan did not include harming or officially deposing Elizabeth herself.

On 7 February, the Lord Chamberlain's Men performed *Richard II* at the Globe Theatre. Although it had been years since *Richard II* had last appeared on the London stage, the conspirators persuaded the players with a bonus of 40 shillings beyond the normal rate. Conspicuous by its inclusion in that day's performance was the so-called deposition scene. This episode, in Act IV of the play, shows the crown changing hands from the deposed Richard to Henry. The deposition scene had been censored, as too politically inflammatory, from all three printings in the 1590s. An oft-quoted story, perhaps apocryphal, is that after hearing of this commissioned performance, Elizabeth remarked to her archivist, 'I am Richard II! Know ye not that?'

The next day, Essex and his accomplices made their move. But they were unable to rouse Londoners to their cause. Robert Cecil dispersed the few hundred followers of Essex by having heralds declare the Earl a traitor. Essex had surrendered by day's end. By month's end, Essex and four co-conspirators had been found guilty of treason and executed. The Earl of Southampton, although found guilty of treason, was sentenced to life imprisonment in the Tower of London. Southampton would be freed by James in one of his first acts after his accession to the English throne. What's more, the king granted Southampton the monopoly on sweet wine, the very same concession that Elizabeth had fatefully denied to the Earl of Essex a few years prior.

James, once he was King of England, also made a point of favouring the late Earl of Essex's twelve-year-old son. In a typically Jacobean public display of affection, James took the boy in his arms, kissed him, and loudly declared him 'the son of the most noble knight that English lad has ever begotten'. Furthermore, he made the Essex boy his sword bearer for the official royal entrance into London. James also arranged for the young Essex to be one of Prince Henry's royal buddies.

The aftermath of the Essex affair was the Cecil faction's total domination of the Privy Council. This turned out to be the best possible outcome for James because the incident had convinced Cecil of the need to settle the succession question once and for all. Although Robert Cecil had inherited his father's distrust of James, he recognized that the King of Scots was the obvious choice to succeed Elizabeth. James had experience as a monarch, after all, and was clearly a competent one at that. Plus he had two sons and a daughter, which would be a welcome relief from all of the uncertainty regarding succession when the time came for James to die. Furthermore, choosing James eliminated him as a threat – the opposite of what would result from any other choice of successor. Thence forward, Elizabeth's government considered James the future King of England. This was kept secret – not only from the public, but from Elizabeth herself.

To that end, Cecil and James carried on a secret correspondence up until Elizabeth's death, to plan for the transition and to keep James informed of developments at Elizabeth's court. In these letters, they even used a code whereby key government individuals were each referred to by a different number – for example, James was '30' and Robert Cecil was '10'. Cecil avoided a close call on one particular occasion when the aged queen noticed that there was diplomatic correspondence from Scotland and asked to see it. Cecil told her that the diplomatic bag containing the letters stank from horse dung, and that he would show them to Her Majesty after they had been aired. Fortunately for Cecil, and perhaps for James, this explanation satisfied her.

James had certainly been fortunate when sending a pair of diplomats to negotiate as ambassadors to Essex. These two, James's childhood friend John Erskine, Earl of Mar, and Edward Bruce, Lord Kinloss, had set off from Edinburgh, but Essex had been executed before they reached London. James was able to communicate to them that they must change tack to 'walk surely between the precipices of the Queen and the people'. The result was a meeting with Cecil, wherein he agreed to do all in his immense power to ensure that James became the next King of England. It was also agreed that

James would not seek parliamentary recognition of his claim to the throne.

The arrangement was of mutual benefit to James and Cecil. James secured his succession and could relax about it. Just in time, too. James had begun to lose his trademark calculating patience regarding the succession and had started considering clearly rash actions, such as raising an army to back up his claim with force. Cecil meanwhile ensured not only that he would have a place in the next regime, but that he would be immediately indispensable.

The Union of the Crowns

Early in the morning of 24 March 1603, the moment that James had been waiting, planning, and hoping for finally arrived: Elizabeth shuffled off this mortal coil. It is unlikely that rigor mortis had even begun to set in before Cecil and the Privy Council proclaimed him King James I of England. The Tudor dynasty had come to an end, and the Stuart dynasty, founded in Scotland in 1371, had expanded to England. Hoping to prevent an insurrection, Cecil and his operatives added extra security in and around London, closed the ports, and kept a close watch on rival claimants such as Arabella Stuart, Lord Beauchamp, and the Earl of Hertford. As it turned out, the precautions were unnecessary.

James had arrived at this point, according to Susan Doran, by a mixture of skill and good fortune:

> By winning over Cecil and other English noblemen James made sure of the succession; no rival candidate reared his or her head; no parliament was called to choose a successor.

> James came to the throne by right of legitimacy, a right declared unambiguously in the 1604 Act of Recognition.
>
> So in the event, the Elizabethan question ended with 'with a whimper, not a bang'. Few, however, had anticipated such a smooth and painless transition to a new dynasty, and unless we unfairly dismiss James's anxieties as paranoia and the uncertainties of many Englishmen as neurotic, we have to accept that the succession issue remained of public interest and concern until Elizabeth's death. There might well have been a different outcome. James was lucky: Thomas Seymour had died in 1600; William Stanley married into Cecil's family; Lord Beauchamp had no interest in the throne; and Arabella Stuart ruined any chances she might have had by her erratic behaviour in 1602 and 1603. Furthermore, Essex's disgrace and later execution brought James the opportunity to mend fences with Cecil and stop the succession dispute becoming a tool of faction. (Doran, 2006, p. 42)

While Doran's point regarding James's luck is well taken, no other potential candidate dedicated anywhere near as much time, energy, resources, and focus as did the King of Scots.

James travelled slowly through England toward London, staying at various nobles' houses and hunting everywhere he went. This period of time was surely one of the happiest of his life. All of the planning, scheming, calculating, manipulating, and grovelling had finally paid off. He'd won the game of thrones, if you will.

He did learn a few of the wrong lessons during his southward trip through his new kingdom. Unfortunately, he mistook for love the people's relief at the peaceful transition. Anxiety regarding the succession had been growing in England with every passing year. The fear – stoked in no small part by the history plays of Shakespeare – was that rival claimants to the throne would back up their claims with force, thus dragging England into civil war. Hence, there was a national outpouring of relief as people realized that their worst fears wouldn't come to pass, and James was greeted by joyous and increasingly larger crowds wherever he went.

He also assumed that England was richer than it was, since he mistook the extraordinary displays of wealth put on for his benefit as normal for the English nobility. In reality, every extra day that James and his entourage spent at any given great house typically put enormous strain on all but the richest of families. His hosts were confident that hosting their new king would pay off handsomely down the road. Often, however, they lived in quiet, desperate hope that the royal visit would end as soon as possible.

In fact, England's finances weren't in particularly good order at the time of Elizabeth's death. Years of war with Spain, not to mention protracted rebellion in Ireland, had syphoned off resources. The English crown was actually in debt to the tune of 400,000 pounds. The fledgling colonial adventure in the New World had yet to become the cash cow that would support empire. James would be disabused of his notions of grandeur soon enough, but for now, it was party time.

The First Week

Within a week of arriving in London, James had promoted the Lord Chamberlain's Men to the King's Men, officially proclaiming the theatre company to be the official court players. Royal demand for their services would see an immediate and sustained increase under James. While the Lord Chamberlain's

Men averaged just over three plays per year at Queen Elizabeth's court, the King's Men averaged well over thirteen plays per year at King James's court.

ACT IV

His Majesty's Little Beagle

As mentioned earlier, Robert Cecil was the second-born son of William Cecil, Lord Burghley, the Machiavellian *consigliere* to Queen Elizabeth. Deemed to have the right stuff to be a statesman (which his older brother apparently lacked), Robert was groomed by his father to take over the family business of being close advisor to the monarch. Hunchbacked since infancy – purportedly due to being dropped on his head by a wet nurse – Robert emerged as the consummate early modern statesman.

Centuries before George W. Bush, King James delighted in bestowing affectionate pet names on his underlings. Surely one of the more humiliating of these was what he most frequently (but by no means solely) used to refer to his closest advisor: 'beagle'. More often than not, it was 'little beagle'. Indeed, letter after letter from the king to Robert Cecil, addressing matters of state, bore the salutation: 'My little beagle'.

Nonetheless, King James and his secretary of state were an ideal match. James wanted someone else to handle the constant bothers of government, and Cecil was only too happy to oblige. Cecil, with a hand in everything, had tremendous power in the day-to-day government of the realm. Notably, while his father had mentored and groomed him, Robert did not train anyone to replace him, so his death in 1612 would have profound consequences for James's government.

The Hampton Court Conference and the King James Version of the Bible

In January 1604, over a period of three days, James met with representatives of the Church of England at his palace at Hampton Court. The Hampton Court Conference was set up in response to a Puritan petition for reform. James tended to view Puritans as a threat to his authority, and to order and stability generally. In fact, he quite consistently treated the Puritans as more of a threat to his regime than Catholics, which is quite remarkable in light of the events to come in November 1605. In typical Jacobean fashion, the king was able to get his way on all of the important points while leaving the Puritans satisfied, at least temporarily, that they had obtained significant concessions.

An important legacy of the Hampton Court Conference was the agreement to produce a translation of the Bible into English – the Authorized Version or, as it is commonly known, the King James Version. The Puritans, who were close readers of the Bible, had become very dissatisfied with the existing translations. A new translation had thus been one of their key demands at Hampton Court. Forty-seven scholars, divided into six committees (two teams each from Cambridge, Oxford, and London), were set to work on the translation.

However, even this 'victory' played into the king's hands. James gave the translators a number of instructions, many of which limited Puritan influence on the translation. When all was said and done, James had bamboozled the Puritans into believing they had wrung concessions out of the king, whereas he had actually conceded very little.

A Counterblaste to Tobacco

Almost four hundred years ahead of his time, James published the anti-tobacco screed *A Counterblaste to Tobacco*, in 1604. At the time, tobacco was all the rage. *A Counterblaste* contains the far-and-away most quoted line in all of the king's works. He describes tobacco as (transliterated into modern English):

> A custom loathsome to the eye, hateful to the nose, harmful to the brain, dangerous to the lungs, and in the black stinking fume thereof, nearest resembling the horrible Stigian smoke pit that is bottomless.

Parliaments, Addled and Otherwise

James never really got along with his English parliaments, pretty well from the start. No one came to blows (unlike what ensued under the rule of his much less capable son, Charles I, who ended up on the chopping block after a bloody civil war). Nevertheless, throughout his English reign, the relationship between the king and his parliaments was an exercise in mutual frustration.

The English parliament was then, as the UK parliament remains today, made up of the House of Lords and the House of Commons, but the monarch had the power to call and dissolve parliaments at will. Parliament had two main functions and prerogatives. First, only parliament could make new statutes, although the king could veto any bills. Second, parliament could grant taxes; from the fourteenth century, these also had to receive the consent of the House of Commons. James was not used to a parliament with rights such as the English parliament had carved out for itself. Although Scotland had a similar institution, called a General Assembly, it was completely subordinate to the monarch's will. James was never really able to wrap his head around the whole idea of a parliament that could defy the monarch's wishes. As far as he was concerned, parliament should be no different than any other part of the government – there to do his bidding.

The 1604 parliament marked the end of the honeymoon period, when everyone was utterly relieved to have avoided bloodshed over the succession. James had two main aims for this first session:

1. the approval of funds sufficient for the running of his household and the state;
2. the permanent legal union of England and Scotland.

James expected that it would be little more than a formality for parliament to agree to these two goals. Instead, he ended up proroguing parliament, in frustration, having failed to convince them to agree on either matter. The House of Commons further refused, on legal grounds, to grant him the title of 'King of Great Britain'. (He subsequently assumed the title himself by proclamation but was prohibited from using it in legal documents.) The failed parliament ended with James haughtily scolding the assembled parliamentarians as if they were aspiring chefs on one of those god-awful cooking shows. In his closing speech, he said: 'I will not thank where I feel no thanks due . . . I am not of such a stock as to praise fools . . . You see how many things you did not well . . . I wish you make use of your liberty with more modesty in time to come' ("James VI and I and the English Parliament," n.d.).

James would periodically call this parliament to session from 1604 until 1611, at which time he dissolved it in complete frustration. He didn't call another until 1614. This second parliament, which lasted for fewer than eight weeks, is known as 'The Addled Parliament'; it, too, got nothing accomplished, although it took considerably less time to do nothing than the previous one. Upon dissolving that one, James said he was 'amazed that his ancestors should have allowed such an institution to come into existence' ("Addled Parliament," n.d.). It would be much the same with the other two parliaments he called, in 1620–22 and 1623–25. Despite the fact that the final one, which dissolved upon his death, was called 'The Happy Parliament' by a contemporary commentator, it was plagued with the same mutual mistrust present in all of the previous three.

The Gunpowder Plot

'Remember, remember, the fifth of November, the gunpowder treason and plot'. So begins a common variant of a Guy Fawkes ditty, a verse commemorating the failure of an alleged coup attempted early in James's English reign. Apart, perhaps, from the publication of the King James Version of the Bible, the Gunpowder Plot is probably the event for which the reign of James is best known today. The story goes that a group of Catholic conspirators planned to blow up the House of Lords during the State Opening of Parliament on 5 November 1605. Had events gone according to plan, the king, most of the royal family, and parliament would have died, and a popular revolt would then have been fomented in the Midlands, with the ultimate goal of installing James's nine-year-old daughter, Princess Elizabeth, and raising her as a Catholic (the rest of the royal family, including Princes Henry and Charles, were expected to be in attendance on opening day and hence killed in the explosion).

The conspirators were betrayed, it would seem, by their own Catholic loyalties. Wishing to warn fellow Catholic William Parker, 4th Baron Monteagle, they sent him an anonymous letter advising him to skip the opening day of parliament. Parker handed the letter over to Robert Cecil. Shortly thereafter, Guy Fawkes was allegedly discovered in an undercroft of the House of Lords. Also in the undercroft was enough gunpowder to blow the building and all of its inhabitants to kingdom come. For his efforts, William Parker received from the Crown 500 pounds in cash and 200 pounds' worth of land. For their efforts, Fawkes and eight co-conspirators were hanged, drawn, and quartered.

As he had done with the Gowrie Plot, James commemorated his 'safe delivery' by making 5 November a national holiday. The *Observance of 5th November Act 1605* was passed by parliament in early 1606, and the law wasn't repealed until March 1859, as part of the *Anniversary Days Observation Act*. Some Britons still observe the tradition of lighting a bonfire on what's usually known as Guy Fawkes Night, Guy Fawkes Day, or Bonfire Night.

Robert Carr

In 1607, at a tilting (jousting) match, James, for the second time in his life, fell in love at first sight. A young, handsome, and charismatic Scot named Robert Carr fell from his horse and broke his leg. James helped to nurse him back to health, teaching him Latin in the process. Carr would receive the proverbial 'royal treatment', with James lavishing titles, lands, and various other goodies on a man who would prove to be a most ungrateful recipient of these favours.

As usual, this preferential status generated a great deal of resentment amongst other courtiers, particularly English members of the court, who were already aggrieved by the prominence of Scots in the king's inner circle. Another consequence was to breed, in Carr, arrogance, ingratitude, and contempt for James. There was not much to like about Carr. The entire royal family, other than the infatuated James, despised the pretty-boy Scotsman.

Carr would eventually fall from favour, with James finally having had enough of Carr's mistreatment. Shortly thereafter, Carr was embroiled in scandal: he was implicated in the murder of his former secretary and lover, Sir Thomas Overbury ('the favourite's favourite'). Carr's wife, Francis Howard, confessed to poisoning Overbury, but Carr maintained his innocence. Both were found guilty of the murder but were pardoned and released after a few years' confinement to the Tower of London.

ACT V

The Deaths of 1612

This year saw the deaths of two people very close to King James: his 'little beagle' and his elder son, Henry Frederick, Prince of Wales. The forty-nine-year-old Cecil had been in poor health and had died on the way to 'take the waters' in Bath. The eighteen-year-old Henry had been struck down by typhoid fever. Both were terrible losses for James. The death of his son devastated him emotionally, while the loss of the competent, dependable Cecil was a massive blow to the smooth running of his kingdoms, divided the court into factions and made the king more dependent upon favourites.

Although there are no stories of the ghost of Henry haunting any particular castles, a mentally unstable man did streak the mourners at Henry's funeral, yelling that he was the dead prince's ghost.

George Villiers

George Villiers was the last of James's three great favourites, and much less problematic than Robert Carr. Well aware of James's particular fondness for pretty boys, courtiers fed up with Carr deliberately contrived for James to become infatuated with Villiers, as a replacement. James did not disappoint, falling deeply in love with the lad and making him the Duke of Buckingham. It was, perhaps, James's most successful personal relationship, not ending in heartache and tragedy, as with Esmé Stuart, or in bitterness and scandal, as with Carr, or even with indifference and neglect, as with his wife, Anna. It certainly seemed to change over time from infatuation and lust to more of a doting, fatherly love. Indeed, in some of his letters to Villiers, James addressed him as 'Sweet and dear child' or signed off as 'Thy dear dad'. Sometimes, however, the sexual partner and the father figure were combined, when he addressed Villiers as 'Sweet child and wife' and signed as 'Thy dear dad and husband' (Norton, 2012). Nevertheless, his relationship with Villiers remained a loving one up until James's death.

One contemporary, John Oglander, whom James knighted in 1615 wrote that James 'loved young men, his favourites, better than women, loving them beyond the love of men to women. I never saw any fond husband make so much or so great dalliance over his beautiful spouse as I have seen King James over his favourites, especially the Duke of Buckingham' (Bergeron, 1999, p. 107). The poet Theophile de Vlau described the relationship between the king and his favourite somewhat less poetically when he included the following line in a contemporary poem: 'And it is well known that the King of England fucks the Duke of Buckingham' ("Personal relationships of James VI and I," n.d.).

Well liked by the entire royal family (unlike Carr), Villiers was also a favourite of Prince Charles. Villiers outlived James but was killed by a rogue army officer a few years later. To the shock and dismay of King Charles, practically the entire nation rejoiced at the murder, since by that time Villiers was widely despised.

'1613–1625: Nothing but Silence'

'1613–1625: Nothing but Silence' is the title of the last chapter of *Royal Family, Royal Lovers*, a book by David Bergeron that examines the life of James particularly through the lens of his closest relationships. The chapter deals with life in the royal family after the death of Prince Henry. Bergeron described the situation thus:

> Terms, relationships, and familial structure changed in this last period of James' life: a period not dominated by achievement or fruition of careful efforts but rather as a time of sadness and disappointment mixed with a residue of tragedy. (Bergeron, 1999, p. 124)

This time was also a transition for James from depending upon Robert Cecil to manage state affairs to relying more and more on his youthful favourite, George Villiers.

Exactly when James started to notice a decline in his mental capacities we don't know. However, when a team of researchers from the University of Kansas tested James's writing, they found: '[O]ur linguistic analysis demonstrates dramatic changes in written language occurring after 1616' (Williams, Holmes, Kemper, & Marquis, 2003, p. 43). He died of a stroke in 1625.

The Workes of the Most High and Mightie Prince

The Workes of the Most High and Mightie Prince, James, by the grace of God, King of Great Britaine, France, and Ireland, Defender of the Faith, &c. was published in 1616. That it was published in the same year as the collected works of Ben Jonson is, according to Jane Rickard, '[t]he most striking aspect of the relationship of James's *Workes* to contemporary literary culture' (Rickard, 2007, p. 143). Interestingly, Rickard also noted, with respect to the omission of any poetry beyond the sonnets already included in two of James's previously published prose works:

> When James embarked upon the project of producing a collected edition of his works, he decided to include all of his prose works to date. These texts incorporate two poems: one of the scriptural exegeses concludes with a sonnet, and the political treatise *Basilikon Doron* begins with a sonnet. But James decided not to include poetry in its own right, even though he had two volumes' worth of printed poetry, and a considerable number of poems that had never been printed. Contemporary comments suggest that the King was still thought of as a poet and that this omission was therefore noticed. (Rickard, 2007, p. 145)

The First Folio

In 1623, *Mr. William Shakespeares Comedies, Histories, & Tragedies* was published by Edward Blount and Isaac Jackard. This volume is usually referred to today as the 'First Folio' – since it was the first of a number of editions of Shakespeare's works that were printed in folio format. Folio format, from the Latin *folium* (leaf), was a method of formatting a book by folding the sheet of paper only once, and was reserved for high-quality, expensive volumes. Quarto format, on the other hand, wherein the sheet was folded into four quarters, was used for cheaper publications. While some of the plays of Shakespeare had been printed previously in quarto editions, this was the first time the plays had been gathered together and published in folio format.

Mayerne's Medical Report

Theodore De Mayerne, a Swiss Huguenot, became the principal physician to the royal family in 1611. In 1623, in preparation for an extended absence from court, Mayerne produced a detailed medical history of King James for use by physicians in his absence. Peters and colleagues (2012) translated this report from its original Latin and used it as the basis to create the following list of 'principal medical symptoms and events of James VI/I':

> Dysfunctional childhood
> Delayed walking until 5–7 years with persistent lower limb weakness
> Persistent movement and behaviour disorders
> 'Tongue too large for mouth'; speech and swallowing difficulties

Delicate itchy skin
Scanty beard
Recurrent renal colic with 'blood-red crumbly sand' and 'burning of urine'
Gouty arthritis, particularly big toe of left foot
Alcohol misuse
Possibly bisexual
Prone to 'hypochondriac melancholy'
Intellectual decline from c. 1619 (Peters, Garrard, Ganesan, & Stephenson, 2012, p. 281)

CHARACTER/BELIEFS/ATTITUDES

JAMES WAS A COMPLEX MAN, and for centuries, historians have taken a dim view of him. Many have accepted at face value the caricature of James as 'the wisest fool in Christendom', bestowed upon him by the Englishman Anthony Weldon, who was pissed off at James for sacking him after the king learned of disparaging remarks Weldon had made about Scots. Regrettably, much of the distaste for James can likely be chalked up to simple homophobia. Nevertheless, scholarship over the last fifty years or so has developed a much more positive view of King James. Regardless of vantage point, all commentators now agree that he was a witty, highly intelligent, and profoundly learned man.

James was aware of his cleverness and confident in his own mental capacities. He was adept at 'reading' people and could very quickly size up a man's character, including his strengths, weaknesses, and hidden motives. He was a shrewd and wily politician, displaying flexibility and patience to ensure that his interests were protected, and his options remained open, regardless of how events unfolded. He was a master of dissimulation. He was superlatively skilled at manipulation as well as debate – both handy skills in politics. King James was, therefore, a particularly frustrating political opponent (Wormald, 1983, p. 188).

James has often been thought of as lazy, both by contemporaries and by subsequent historians. The enormous amount of time he spent hunting, together with reading, writing, and carousing, is often compared unfavourably with the amount of time he spent on government business. However, recent scholarship has tended to modify that view somewhat, at least in terms of the actual output that James was able to achieve. He was effective by entrusting much of the day-to-day business to capable men like Robert Cecil. He was able to set up a system whereby government business could be conducted even when he was on the hunt. And he was simply more efficient than most people; by his own estimation, James could accomplish the equivalent of five men in any given period of time. Even allowing for a certain amount of braggadocio, his intellect and linguistic mastery clearly support his claim of superiority.

Regardless of how industrious James may have been, one thing is certain: he was constantly in financial trouble. Throughout his life, from the time he was a young king in Scotland until he was an old king of all Britain, he was chronically short of money. This meant his ministers were always scrambling to come up with ways of filling the treasury, but no matter how much money came in, James always managed to see that it went out just as quickly. Some of the problem was that James undoubtedly loved to live the 'good life'. However, the greatest contributor to his constant financial woes was that James saw *largesse* as both an essential perquisite and a duty of the monarch, in the form of distributing wealth to various members of the ruling class. He may also have believed that friends had to be bought.

Much has been made, naturally, about the fact that, from infancy, he was raised in an environment without a lot of love. This upbringing seems to have created in James a desperate, primal need to be loved. Such insecurity can be detected in each of his relationships with his various favourites. It may also help to explain the king's seeming inability to say no to suitors and, therefore, his *largesse* problem.

James had a huge capacity for love. Indeed, it can easily be said that he was 'one that loved not wisely but too well'. Bluntly, James liked pretty boys. Ever since he had recovered from his adolescent crush on his much older cousin, Esmé Stuart, James's head was consistently turned by attractive young men, with whom he often fell madly in love. He would lavish attention and treasures upon these favourites. James's relationships with favourites caused problems for him, not just financially but because they invariably would become the subject of envy and resentment from others in the court. Furthermore, James had difficulty ending relationships, even after they had become toxic. In the words of G.P.V. Akrigg (1984), 'once he had given his heart, he found it a torment to withdraw it'. Robert Carr had the temerity to treat James with open contempt. Such situations do tend to diminish the majesty of a monarch.

James was averse to war, taking *Beati Pacifici* ('blessed are the peacemakers')[4] as his personal motto. He also proclaimed himself *Rex Pacificus* ('King of Peace' or 'Peaceful King'). It wasn't a disingenuous gesture, either. He avoided going to war until the last year of his life, when he was pressured into

---

4. The Latin form of the first half of Matthew 5:9, the seventh verse of the Sermon on the Mount.

declaring war with Spain after his son Charles bungled an attempt to marry the Infanta. Otherwise, the closest he had ever come to even preparing for battle had been clandestinely building an army at the turn of the seventeenth century, in case he had to back up his claim to the English throne with force. Immediately upon ascending to the English throne, he took steps to end the war with Spain that Elizabeth I had been waging since 1585, signing the Treaty of London in 1604. Later in his English reign, he styled himself as a peacemaker on the European stage, although he was unsuccessful in trying to stop what would become the calamitous Thirty Years' War.

James conducted governmental and courtly business in a relaxed, informal manner. While this had proven particularly effective for his rule in Scotland, it caused some friction with the English, who were used to Elizabeth's aloof formality. James also preferred to treat his servants in a familiar, jocular, kind manner. A telling incident occurred when the king had kicked his elderly servant for losing some important papers. After James found out that the loss had been his own fault, he got down on his knees to beg the servant's forgiveness.

One shouldn't mistake this relatively humane treatment of servants to mean that James was a man of the people. Far from it. In an oft-quoted report from 1607, the Venetian ambassador opines that James did not 'caress the people, nor make them that good cheer the late Queen did, whereby she won their loves'. Indeed, another contemporary of James noted: 'The access of the people made him so impatient that he often dispersed them with frowns, and on being told that they only wished to see his face, he cried out, "God's wounds! I will pull down my breeches and they shall also see my arse."' Although he was not completely indifferent to the plight of the common man, it was really only through service that a commoner could prove worthy of his notice.

James's personality structure can be thought of as a sort of mirror-image of his childhood tutor, George Buchanan. While Buchanan had a highly developed humanist political philosophy intellectually, he was a highly authoritarian bully personally. James, on the other hand, had a highly developed authoritarian political theory intellectually, while he was a sensitive, personable, quite affable fellow personally. Furthermore, although James was certainly capable of vindictiveness and even cruelty at times, he was generally a forgiving and merciful king. His undeniable playfulness shines through in many letters to various favourites and, of course, to his 'little beagle', Cecil.

James was a sucker for flattery. He certainly encouraged courtiers and suitors to heap lavish praise on him. This is usually explained, justifiably, with reference to the lack of love in his childhood. Such an explanation is completely sufficient for explaining James's proclivity for flattery, of course. And how much explanation does being susceptible to flattery need, really? Nevertheless, I wonder whether he didn't also encourage flattery as a means of sizing up a man's character and motives. After all, not only was James an excellent judge of character, but he also generally had a keen sense of his own strengths and weaknesses. Whether or not he did so consciously, James would have obtained valuable information about a man's character by observing him in the act of flattery.

There were three historical figures with whom James chose to publicly and favourably compare and associate himself: King Solomon, Caesar Augustus, and Henry VII. He liked to think of himself as having the wisdom of Solomon – a great patriarch of the Old Testament. He wanted his subjects to see him as a father figure whose superior judgement would lead his nation as wisely and justly as Solomon had done his people.

He associated himself with Caesar Augustus as a founding father of a great empire – Augustus with the Roman Empire, James with the British Empire. For example the medal struck in 1603 to commemorate his coronation in England had, on the 'heads' side, the inscription 'IAC : I : BRIT : CAE : AVG : HAE CEASVM CAE. D. D'., which was abbreviated Latin for 'James I, Caesar Augustus of Britain, Caesar the heir of the Caesars, presents this medal'. James's conception of empire had more to do with his unification of Great Britain rather than the massive overseas colonial empire we think of today when using the term 'British Empire'. As it turns out, however, James can be thought of as a founding father, so to speak, of the British Empire. For better or for worse, the Ulster plantation, Jamestown, Virginia, and Nova Scotia (Latin for 'New Scotland'), for example, were all founded during his monarchy and were the seeds that would grow to become Northern Ireland, as well as parts of the United States and Canada, respectively.

Finally, he associated himself with Henry VII because James's claim to the English throne derived from that predecessor. When James made his triumphant ceremonial entrance into London in 1604, the triumphal arch under which he passed bore artwork showing an image of King James, mounted on horseback, receiving a sceptre from Henry VII. He boasted to his new English subjects, in his first address to parliament, that whereas Henry VII had united England by bringing together the two great houses of York and Lancaster, he had united the two great nations of England and Scotland to create the kingdom of Britain.

When even the brightest mind in our world has been trained up from childhood in a superstition of any kind, it will never be possible for that mind, in its maturity, to examine sincerely, dispassionately, and conscientiously any evidence or any circumstance which shall seem to cast a doubt upon the validity of that superstition. I doubt if I could do it myself.
—Mark Twain, "Is Shakespeare Dead? From My Autobiography"

THREE | The Evidence

Looney's *Shakespeare Identified* Criteria

J. Thomas Looney was a schoolmaster from the north of England. In the early twentieth century, Looney had become interested in the Shakespeare authorship question. The Baconian theory had, by that time, become more and more focussed on cryptographic explanations tying the works of Shakespeare to Bacon and his ideas. Convinced that Bacon was as unlikely to be the author as William Shakspere of Stratford was, Looney decided to take a more methodical, scientific approach to the search for the true author.

To that end, he developed a methodology of, essentially, looking at the works for clues as to what type of person to seek as the author, using those clues as criteria to discern suitable candidates, and then comparing the characteristics of any suitable candidate(s) to the works of Shakespeare. Looney's method produced, of course, Edward de Vere, the Earl of Oxford, as the final candidate for Shakespeare authorship. Despite what I believe to be an erroneous result, the criteria Looney developed are quite sound. Indeed, had Looney not made one crucial, albeit understandable, error, it's quite plausible that he would have identified James rather than de Vere.

The first step that Looney took was to 'examine the works of Shakespeare, almost as though they had appeared for the first time, unassociated with the name or personality of any writer, and from such an examination draw what inferences we could as to his character and circumstances' (Looney, 1920, p. 81). From this, he identified nine 'General Features' and nine 'Special Characteristics'. What happens if we compare James to Looney's eighteen criteria? As you'll see, the result is a close match.

General Features

1. *Recognized genius and mysterious / A mature man of recognized genius*

King James was most certainly 'a man of recognized and recorded genius'. His contemporaries recognized his impressive intellect, and his genius is apparent from the history books. In discussing the potential consequences of his intellect being put to use in secret to write the works of Shakespeare, Looney commented: 'a man who has produced so large an amount of work of the highest quality, and was not seen doing it, must have passed a considerable part of his life in what would appear to others like doing nothing of any consequence' (Looney, 1920, p. 85). That's exactly what James was accused of by contemporaries and subsequent historians.

2. *Appearance of eccentricity / apparently eccentric and mysterious*
Looney wrote that 'the whole manner of his anonymity marks the writer as being, in a manner, something of an eccentric: his nature, or his circumstances, or probably both, were not normal' (Looney, 1920, p. 85). Self-evidently, being the King of Scots qualifies as an abnormal circumstance. Nevertheless, James was mysterious even by monarchical standards, with a reputation for being one of the world's most secretive princes.

3. *A man apart / of intense sensibility*
James was, indeed, an intensely sensitive fellow. With respect to being 'a man apart', the nature of monarchy essentially guaranteed his separateness, regardless of any particular personality traits.

4. *Unconventional*
Aside from being unlike everyone else in the kingdom, simply by virtue of being the monarch, King James was also extraordinarily unconventional when compared to other monarchs of the period. For instance, conventionally, monarchs did not publish literary works. James broke the mould in this respect.

5. *Apparent inferiority to requirements of the work / not adequately appreciated*
Looney saw this criterion as essentially following from the identification of a person, hitherto not thought of as the author, as 'Shakespeare'. Nevertheless, it seems particularly applicable

to King James, as the following quote from *Great Britain's Solomon* attests:

> His unbusinesslike lifestyle and the disorderly nature of his court, both so very different from Elizabeth's, concealed the amount of attention he paid to business and have given him a reputation for laziness that is far from deserved. (Lee, 1990, p. 111)

6. An Englishman of literary tastes / of pronounced and known literary tastes

Looney confined his search to native-born Englishmen, based on the following logic: 'His writings being masterpieces of English literature, and all the world's literary masterpieces having been produced by men who wrote in their mother-tongue' (Looney, 1920, p. 87). This was the fatal flaw in Looney's methodology. It was not a particularly unreasonable assumption, given when Looney was writing, just after the end of World War I. *Heart of Darkness* had been written, for example, but it was not yet considered a masterpiece. The novel by Polish-born Joseph Conrad did not receive anything like the recognition it enjoys today until after World War II. Nabokov's *Lolita* had yet to be written, and Tom Stoppard had yet to be born. It thus seems reasonable for Looney to have assumed that the playwright was an Englishman. By doing so, however, he foreclosed the possibility of considering James as a candidate. Consequently, Looney may have gone looking for Hamlet at the wrong court in the British Isles.

In discussing the nature of the author's pronounced and known literary tastes, Looney ventured: 'Other interests he may have had, just as men who were chiefly occupied with social and political affairs, dabbled also in literature, poetry, or the drama; but what to them was a mere hobby or pastime would be to him a central and consuming purpose' (Looney, 1920, p. 87). This fits James to a tee. After all, James had confessed to the Bishop of Zealand that he had been addicted to the literary arts from his earliest days. Even without this confession, his passion for literature is quite apparent from a close study of the man and his life.

He understood how powerful was his mastery of language and writing. Jane Rickard explores precisely this understanding in *Authorship and Authority: The Writing of James VI and I*. She explains:

> The present book argues that all of James's writings, including his religious and political prose works, are to a large extent the product of his interest in the ability of art to manipulate and deceive, and of his self-consciousness about the relationship between authors, texts, and readers. While these issues arise not only in relation to literature but also in relation to other rhetorical uses of language, James seems have developed this interest and self-consciousness through his early experiences with poetry in particular. For though in the 1580s he was also reading and beginning to write in other genres, he was especially concerned with reading, translating, collaborating, and writing within the arena of poetry, and this is the period in which his authorial aims and concerns began to take shape. He seems to have become acutely aware of the power of art, of writing as a central means of establishing his authority, and perhaps even of the extent to which his authority depended upon effective representation. He was likewise aware that others might use this power against him, and was therefore concerned to guide, respond to, or censor other writers. (Rickard, 2007, p. 18)

7. Dramatic interests / An enthusiast in the world of drama

This criterion is unquestionably applicable to James. He invited acting companies to visit Scotland no fewer than four times, in 1589, 1594, 1599, and 1601. He'd written material for the Huntley wedding masque. He even incorporated dramatic elements into his prose work – for example, by structuring *Daemonologie* as a dialogue. Furthermore, there is no greater demonstration of the priority James placed upon theatre and the stage than the letters patent creating the *King's Men*, one of his very first acts of state.

8. A lyric poet of recognized talent

James adored poetry and wrote it throughout his life, although he only published it outside of the years 1591–1618. Even during this intervening time, he couldn't help adding an introductory sonnet to *Basilikon Doron*. James was not only a lyric poet, generally, he was a sonneteer, particularly, and consistently favoured that form.

9. Classical education / of superior education / the habitual associate of educated people

James had one of the best educations available to Europeans at the time. He loved intellectual conversation, revelling in debating the finer points of theology at the supper table. He sought out learned discussion wherever he went. His honeymoon in Denmark is a good example of this quest for knowledge, as during that time he discussed Copernican theory and cosmology with Tycho Brahe and Calvinism with Niels Hemmingsen.

Special Characteristics

10. His feudal partialities / a man with feudal connections
Looney, calling Shakespeare 'essentially a medievalist', wrote:

> [W]hen, therefore, we find that the great Shakespearean plays were written at a time when men were revelling in what they considered to be a newly-found liberation from Medievalism, it is evident that Shakespeare was one whose sympathies, and probably his antecedents, linked him more closely to the old order than to the new: not the kind of man we should expect to rise from the lower middleclass population of the towns. (Looney, 1920, pp. 93–94)

This indubitably applies to King James. His dynastic house, the House of Stuart/Stewart, had ruled Scotland since 1371. The name comes from the fact that previous ancestors had held the medieval office of High Steward of Scotland since the thirteenth century.

11. Aristocratic outlook / a member of the higher aristocracy
Under this category, regarding Shakespeare's aristocratic point of view, Looney wrote: '[W]e feel entitled, therefore, to claim for Shakespeare high social rank, and even a close proximity to royalty itself' (Looney, 1920, p. 95). Indeed.

12. Lancastrian leanings / connected with Lancastrian supporters
James's claim to the English throne was based upon descent from Henry VII – who, we remember, was the leader of the victorious Lancastrian forces at the Battle of Bosworth Field. Henry VII's claim to the throne was based upon descent from the Duke of Lancaster (John of Gaunt). James wore his descent

'from the loins of Henry VII' on his sleeve, so to speak. Therefore, he clearly had Lancastrian connections.

13. Enthusiast for Italy

Including plays set in ancient Rome, fourteen of Shakespeare's plays have some or all of the action set in Italy (*All's Well that Ends Well, Antony and Cleopatra, Coriolanus, Cymbeline, Julius Caesar, Merchant of Venice, Much Ado About Nothing, Othello, Romeo and Juliet, The Taming of the Shrew, Titus Andronicus, The Two Gentleman of Verona,* and *The Winter's Tale*). Looney asserted (ironically using as an example the one foreign country that James had visited), '[W]e feel that these plays carry us to Italy in a way that "Hamlet" never succeeds in carrying us to Denmark' (Looney, 1920, p. 96). Whether or not we buy into this wholly subjective assertion, there is no question that the playwright was enthusiastic about Italy.

Supporters of the Oxfordian theory tend to emphasize the Italian angle – as well they should, since de Vere travelled extensively in Italy, supporting the contention that he was the true author. I think some Oxfordians veer into overemphasis, however, when they claim that the descriptions of Italian locations in Shakespeare's plays are so vivid and accurate that the playwright *must* have experienced them first-hand. Surely, even if one is willing to concede that the author of the Shakespeare plays could not have constructed his descriptions of Italy solely from his vast reading, it is equally plausible that he obtained his knowledge second-hand in conversation with people who had seen it first-hand.

King James certainly didn't lack for friends and acquaintances with whom to have such conversations. William Fowler, the translator of Petrarch and Machiavelli, travelled about as extensively in Italy as Edward de Vere. James's Italian tutor,

Castelvetro, not only had grown up in Italy but had travelled around it quite a lot. Another source of first-hand knowledge – of Venice, in particular – would have been the Venetian ambassador to the Jacobean court, with whom the king regularly enjoyed convivial discussion.

The Italian influence upon James's art is undeniable. His favourite poetic form, the sonnet (derived from the Italian word *sonetto*, 'little song'), was an Italian invention, developed by Petrarch in the late fourteenth century. As mentioned earlier, the masque that James wrote for the Earl of Huntly's wedding displayed familiarity with *commedia dell'arte*, another Italian invention. The influence of *commedia dell'arte* is evident in a number of Shakespeare plays, including *Comedy of Errors*, *The Taming of the Shrew*, and *Love's Labour's Lost* ("Narrative and dramatic sources of all Shakespeare's works," 2008).

A stronger case can be made that the author must have *read* Italian than that he must have travelled in Italy, when one considers that some of Shakespeare's sources were written in Italian, and no English translations were available before the publication of the First Folio, in 1623. For instance, Shakespeare frequently consulted the works of an Italian, Giovanni Battista Giraldi (1504–1573), who went by the nickname 'Cinthio'. *Measure for Measure* borrows from two of Cinthio's works, *Epitia* and *Hecatommithi*. *Othello* is also based on a story from *Hecatommithi*, called 'Disdemona and the Moor'. No English translations of Giraldi's works that Shakespeare could have used have ever been found.

14. Sporting tastes / a follower of sport (including falconry)
By 'sporting tastes', Looney didn't mean football or what we would tend to think of as sports. He means hunting, specifically. James was unequivocally *addicted* to hunting. From his

James, aged 14, with falcon by Unknown artist. Portrait of James VI and I with the "Mirror of Great Britain" jewel in his hat. Scottish National Gallery, obtained from Wikimedia Commons, https://commons.wikimedia.org/wiki/File:James_I_de_Critz_Mirror_of_GB.jpg.

early childhood onward, hunting was an obsession. He hunted in good times and in bad. During the funerals for both his son Henry and his wife, Anna, James was out hunting. James claimed, with a great deal of justification, that the exercise (riding on horseback, usually at full speed) was essential for his health, particularly with respect to his weak legs. Occasions when he was unable to hunt for an extended period of time were often followed by a decrease in his overall health. The king's devotion was so great that his officials sometimes had to downplay notions that all he ever did was hunt, to the detriment of government business.

15. Music / a lover of music

We don't have a great deal of evidence that James was particularly fond of music. In fact, there is a bit of evidence against that. According to De Fontenay, the French emissary sent by Mary, Queen of Scots, in 1584 to report on her then eighteen-year-old son, James 'hates the dance and music in general, like all fopperies of the court'. It's possible that he outgrew this adolescent apparent hatred of music. Nevertheless, it's quite clear that, while there is absolutely no mistaking James's passion for poetry, literature, and hunting, our sources indicate no such passion for music .

Regardless of his personal feelings towards music, he clearly respected and supported it as well as musicians. Music was an integral part of the flourishing art scene encouraged at the Jacobean court. James attracted Thomas and Robert Hudson from the north of England into his 'Castalian Band' specifically for their musical talent, to be court musicians as well as poets.

16. Finances / loose and improvident in money matters

There is not a single period of James's life, from the time he assumed full reign of Scotland as a teenager to his death as 'King of Great Britain', when finances were not a major concern for his government. As we have seen regarding his experience with the Octavians, even when he made a conscious effort to rein in his spending, he was unsuccessful. Looney's criterion hence fits James to a tee.

17. Mixed attitude towards women / doubtful and somewhat conflicting in his attitude to women

This is how, in 1920s England, a polite schoolteacher like Looney would imply homosexuality. The closest Looney came was this paragraph:

> Examining, then, these sonnets, we find that there are, in fact, two sets of them. By far the larger and more important set, embracing no less than one hundred and twenty-six out of a total of one hundred and fifty-four, is addressed to a young man, and express a tenderness which is probably without parallel in the recorded expressions of emotional attachment of one man to another. (Looney, 1920, p. 100)

Homoerotic elements are scattered throughout Shakespeare's works. Previous writers have attempted to deny the evidence that the playwright preferred men. For example, critics would explain away the fact that a great many of the sonnets are quite plainly addressed to a man by suggesting that this was part of a poetical exercise or conceit. That is, the 'narrator' of the poem is a character whom the poet has created and who just happens to desire another man. I'm not sure that argument took them as far as they perhaps thought it did.

It should be noted that application of the term 'homosexual' to early modern individuals is somewhat problematic, in that the term implies an identity that simply was not present in the early modern period. That is, while people today identify as homosexual, and we think in terms of a person having a sexual 'orientation', people of the early modern period didn't have that mindset. That said, there is absolutely no question that James was more attracted sexually to men than to women, although he was not repelled by female sexuality. He also enjoyed ribald and bawdy humour with both sexes. According to Pauline Croft, 'he deplored the double standard of morality that insisted on chastity in women but not men. A husband must ensure his wife's obedience, but should treat her as "the halfe of your selfe"' (Croft, 2003, p. 134).

18. Catholicism and scepticism / of probable Catholic leanings, but touched with scepticism

Over the years, including those during his life, people have sometimes been misled by James's encyclopaedic knowledge of the Bible into thinking that James was a particularly pious man. He was nothing of the sort. He enjoyed theology and the Bible as subjects of intellectual discussion or as literary pursuits. He could also cite scripture for his purpose, and he used biblical imagery to bolster his image, justify his actions, or display his erudition. Beyond that, any attention James paid to religion was strictly political. There is certainly nothing to indicate that he made decisions by consulting scripture, for instance. James is also known for his religious tolerance – he did not care what people thought privately about the spiritual realm, so long as it did not interfere with their obedience to him in the earthly realm.

James wasn't Catholic, although he had been baptized as one. He had fallen in love with a Catholic at the age of thirteen – Esmé Stuart. He respected what he called 'our Mother

Church'. Although an unwavering Protestant, he saw the splitting of Christianity that had resulted from the Reformation as tragic, and he favoured Christian reunification. His reign in Scotland was consistently tolerant, with Catholics welcome at his court. Queen Anna quietly converted to Catholicism in the late 1590s. Even after the Gunpowder Plot, he showed remarkable tolerance toward Catholics, merely obliging them to swear an oath of allegiance to the Crown. In fact, all of this tolerance for Catholics has led some to suspect that James was a 'closet Catholic' (Desmond, 2011).

Hugh Trevor-Roper, addressing what Shakespeare's works tell us about the author's religion, wrote:

> That profound, questioning, universal spirit, which could be so philosophical, so metaphysical, so Platonic, never utters a syllable which suggests a personal religion. Beneath his conformity, he may have been Catholic (but an anti-papal English Catholic); he may have been a Protestant (but certainly not a puritan); he may have been a sceptic. Most probably he was a sceptic. In his comedies he loves this life only; in his tragedies there is no hint of another. All we can say certainly is that, though profoundly concerned with the predicament of man, he never questioned the religion of state. The religion of protest, like the politics of protest, left him cold. (Trevor-Roper, 1962, p. 42)

James was, indeed, a sceptical, anti-puritan Protestant for whom the religion of protest, like the politics of protest, had no draw.

Summary of James's Fitness in Terms of Looney's Criteria

So how well does James line up with Looney's criteria? It depends upon how you count a few of them. At worst, James clearly matches fourteen out of the eighteen. For most of these fourteen, the match is perfect – a bullseye, if you will. Of the remaining four, 'an Englishman of literary tastes' clearly becomes a bullseye if we 'correct' the requirement that he be a native-born Englishman rather than someone fluent in English. 'Enthusiast for Italy' matches, provided it not be required that he travelled in Italy (which, I believe, is not an intended requirement of Looney's, although it could be implied by his comments regarding being 'carried' to Italy but not to Denmark). 'Love of music' suffers, perhaps, from how overwhelmingly well most of the other criteria match James, making it seem less than a proper match. However, besides the one eyewitness opinion regarding the tastes of the young king, the evidence indicates that James was a supporter of music and encouraged it at his court. Looney hedged the final criterion, 'Of probable Catholic leanings, but touched with scepticism', with probability. All of the criteria are properly 'probable' rather than certain, of course, yet Looney gave this particular qualification only to Catholicism. Of all of these clues to the author's identity that Looney saw in the works of Shakespeare, he was least confident that Catholicism was a reliable indicator of the author's true nature. In this respect, the criterion is a match – it's just that James actually fits into that area of uncertainty. Looney suspected that the author was probably Catholic, but presumably wouldn't be surprised to find that he wasn't. As a whole, the eighteen criteria that J. Thomas Looney developed, in *Shakespeare Identified*, to determine the true author of the works of Shakespeare are an astonishingly good fit when applied to King James VI and I.

'Made lame by Fortune's dearest spite'

Shakespeare's works contain enough references to being lame that their frequency has been remarked upon, with some commentators concluding that the author must have been lame. The main evidence for this claim comes from Sonnet 37, addressed to the 'fair youth', which begins:

> As a decrepit father takes delight
> To see his active child do deeds of youth,
> So I, made lame by Fortune's dearest spite,
> Take all my comfort of thy worth and truth;

Edgar has a very similar line in King Lear when he refers to himself as '[a] most poor man made lame by fortune's blows'. Furthermore, in Sonnet 66, the poet refers to his 'strength by limping sway disabled' (University College London Media Relations, 2007).

There is absolutely no question that King James suffered from some form of disability of the legs. This disability is summed up in 'The Nature of King James VI/I's Medical Conditions: New Approaches to the Diagnosis':

> There are consistent reports of delayed walking until the age of 5–7 years, with persistent weakness of his legs throughout his life. Lower limb weakness is said to have precluded running-based sports, and James indulged throughout his life in horse riding. His lower limb weakness and deformity have been interpreted as suggesting musculo-skeletal defects and a movement disorder. (Peters et al., p. 281)

Favourites

Blair Worden's 'Favourites on the English Stage', an in-depth exploration of theatrical representations of royal favourites on the early modern stage, begins as follows:

> If there is a single register of the extent and persistence of the early modern preoccupation with the power of royal favourites, it is the theatre. Favourites are everywhere on the early modern English stage (though their ubiquitousness has generally escaped the attention of literary historians and critics). Their deleterious influence on monarchs is a large theme of dramatic representation from the later sixteenth century to the early eighteenth. It announces itself as a theatrical subject in the early 1590s, amidst the rise of the public theatre, in Marlowe's *Edward II* and the anonymous play *Woodstock*. A decade and a half later the theme has matured, through plays by Ben Jonson, John Marston, Samuel Daniel, George Chapman and John Day. (Worden, 1999, p. 160)
>
> ...
>
> A compelling demonstration of this preoccupation can be found in a simple list of plays from the period in question with 'favourite' in the title: *The Favourite, The Deserving Favourite, The Fair Favourite, The False Favourite, The Great Favourite, The Loyal Favourite, The Ungrateful Favourite, The Unhappy Favourite* and *The Fool Would Be a Favourite.*

Worden adds:

> There is a much larger number of plays which have a character (or more than one character) listed as a 'favourite' among the *dramatis personae*, and another much larger number where favouritism, though not declared as a theme in the title or the preliminary matter, figures prominently in the text. The

favourite is a theatrical type, with a recognizable set of characteristics. (Worden, 1999, p. 160)

Given this ubiquity of theatrical representations of royal favourites during Shakespeare's time, and given Shakespeare's obsession with royalty and royal courts, we would expect to find a fair number of such representations in his plays. Instead, Worden's research produced the following remarkable result:

> One writer is conspicuous by his absence from the list of dramatists eager to dramatize the rule of favourites: Shakespeare. We can grasp the point by setting his *Richard II* beside *Woodstock*, which may have been a source for it, and where the theme of favouritism is so much ampler. In Shakespeare the favourites have minor parts. It is true that the lament of John of Gaunt for 'This royal throne of kings, this sceptred isle' follows the scene which introduces Greene, Bagot and Bushy, and is prompted by the Duke of York's account of the victory won by flattery and 'will' over counsel and of the success of the king's lascivious entourage in 'stopp[ing]' his 'ear'. Yet those revelations are not developed.
>
> With one arguable exception, there are no favourites with major parts in Shakespeare. He might have chosen to make a favourite of Polonius. Yet Claudius, like Shakespeare's other wicked kings – like Richard III, like Macbeth, like Leontes – makes his own way to evil. The arguable exception is to be found in *Henry VIII*, the play Shakespeare wrote late in life with John Fletcher, whose own plays are peopled with favourites. Henry for a time allows too much power to Wolsey, the upstart favourite opposed by the ancient nobility, though the king sees his mistake and recovers from it. When in 1628, a

fortnight before the Duke of Buckingham's assassination, the duke attended a revival of *Henry VIII*, observers remarked on his resemblance to Wolsey, that 'lively type of himself, having governed this kingdome eighteen years, as [Buckingham] that fourteen'. Yet that response tells us about the concerns of the observers, not of Shakespeare.

For there is in Shakespeare none of the appetite for barbed or risky topical allusion, and none of the instinct for political didacticism, that characterize many of his contemporary dramatists. (On the one occasion when he clearly alludes to a contemporary politician – probably Essex – he does not have that politician's standing as a favourite in mind.) (Worden, 1999, p. 171)

It's as if Shakespeare were writing from an entirely different perspective from his fellow playwrights. Resentment towards favourites was strictly reserved for subjects – from a king's perspective, there is no 'problem' with favouritism. It should be noted that, for the period in which the Shakespeare plays were written, King James was able to keep the pleasure of the bedchamber separate from the business of government. As Lee noted, 'From the time of Gray's disgrace in May 1587 to the death of Robert Cecil twenty-five years later none of the handsome young men of whom the king was fond – and they were plentiful – had any political influence' (Lee, 1990, p. 240).

Motherless

Favourites are not the only type of character missing from the Shakespeare canon. While not completely absent, mothers are conspicuously underrepresented in Shakespeare's work. There is a particular lack of loving mothers – no character comes close to a female parental equivalent of Prospero, for instance. Germaine Greer, in *Shakespeare's Wife*, made the following observation:

> Most of Shakespeare's heroes and heroines are motherless. The few mothers who do appear in Shakespeare's plays are anything but motherly, from the cannibal mother Tamora in *Titus Andronicus* to the neurotically affected mother in Juliet, the mother of *Richard III* who curses her womb and the Countess of Rossillion in *All's Well* who simply dislikes her son. At best mothers are ineffectual, like Queen Elizabeth in *Richard III*, Lady Faulconbridge in *King John* and Lady Macduff, and at worst depraved, like Gertrude and Lady Macbeth. (Greer, 2007, p. 41)

Weddings

James *loved* a good wedding, especially when one of his young, attractive male favourites was the groom. James would foot the bill for a lavish celebration. The next day, the king would sit with the couple upon the marital bed and extract intimate details regarding the conjugal activities of the wedding night. *Great Britain's Solomon* contains the following description of this peculiar quirk of the king, as displayed after the marriage of his favourite, Philip Herbert: 'James gave [Philip Herbert] and Lady Susan Vere a lavish wedding – James always enjoyed his favorites' weddings – and "gave them in the morning before they were up a *reveille-matin* in his shirt and his nightgown and spent a good hour with them in the bed or upon, choose which you will believe best"' (Lee, 1990, p. 240). Lee noted, 'As was so often the case, James's affection for his favorite reached its peak immediately after the marriage' (Lee, 1990, p. 241).

This is a peculiarly specific facet of James's sexuality – he was sexually attracted to his young, handsome favourites but seemed to get the most thrill out of their wedding nights (i.e., the favourite's sex with a woman). We have 154 Shakespeare sonnets. The vast majority of these – the first 126, in fact – are often referred to collectively as the 'fair youth' sonnets because they are all addressed to an attractive young man. The first seventeen of these 'fair youth' sonnets are further classified together as the 'procreation sonnets' because the author, who is clearly physically attracted to the youth, argues that the young man should marry and father children because he should pass on his beauty to another generation. What better candidate for author of the procreation sonnets is there than a man who urged his favourites to marry, paid for the wedding, sat on or in the nuptial bed with them, asking prurient questions, and whose affection for them peaked immediately after the marriage? The 'fair youth' sonnets, generally, match James's sexuality. The procreation sonnets, in particular, are a spectacularly close match.

By the way, Philip Herbert is one half of the 'incomparable pair of brethren' to whom the First Folio is dedicated. What's more, the other half of the pair, William Herbert, is the leading candidate for the identity of the 'Mr. W. H'. to whom the sonnets are dedicated. Both brothers were close favourites of James. In fact, Oxford University's Pembroke College was co-founded by King James and William Herbert, 3rd Earl of Pembroke.

Taken as a whole – the sonnets, the homoeroticism throughout the works, the male bonding, the cross-dressing, the weddings – Shakespeare's depiction of sexuality very much mirrors James's life: filled with male camaraderie, homoeroticism, and passion, coupled with a respect for female sexuality, the importance of procreation, and a love of weddings.

Du Bartas

The poet who received the greatest share of James's respect and admiration, especially in his youth, surely was Guillaume Salluste Du Bartas, whom I have mentioned earlier. Du Bartas was clearly influential in the development of the young poet-king's art. If James were the author of Shakespeare's works, we would expect to find evidence of this influence there, particularly in the earlier works. We do. James Fitzgerald, a supporter of the Oxfordian theory of Shakespeare authorship, in the course of research in support of that theory, discovered an interesting connection between Du Bartas and the works of Shakespeare. He'd noticed the use of the phrase 'orient pearl' in an anonymous song that he suspected may have been written by Shakespeare, particularly Shakespeare identified as the Earl of Oxford. Fitzgerald explained:

> Needing to start somewhere, I took down Bartlett's *Familiar Quotations* from the shelf, where I found one entry contemporary to Shakespeare for 'orient pearl', in excerpts from the works of an unfamiliar French poet, Guillaume De Saluste Seigneur Du Bartas (1544–1590). His translator was another stranger, Josuah Sylvester. In the Du Bartas entry, fully one-half of the sum of sixteen cross-referenced citations to echoes of Du Bartas in English Literature went to Shakespeare. Of the remaining citations, all but one were posthumous, both to Oxford and the Stratford man. (Fitzgerald, 1999, p. 76)

Du Bartas wrote in an elaborate style, the French equivalent of a style called euphuism. Hugh Trevor-Roper, describing Shakespeare's style, wrote: 'His early works were deeply influenced by the elaborate, artificial "euphuism" made fashionable by

John Lyly: a style of writing which he first marvellously exploited, then transcended' (Trevor-Roper, 1962, p. 41).

Depictions of Royal Courts

One of the most common points raised by anti-Stratfordians is Shakespeare's apparent insider knowledge of courts and courtly life, displayed in so many of his plays. The usual explanation that Stratfordians give for this is that he observed it first-hand as a player/playwright-servant at the courts of Elizabeth and James. While this explanation may seem plausible enough at first glance, it becomes more and more absurd the earlier the play it is that one considers. The Henry VI series and *Richard III*, for example, were among the very first plays that Shakespeare wrote. Some sources cite *Henry VI, Part II* as the very first play he wrote, in fact. One often reads that the Henry VI plays lack the artistic mastery Shakespeare would later display – a trajectory can be discerned, with the Henry VI trilogy at the bottom of the curve. We would expect to find such a trajectory regarding the playwright's depiction of court life. That is, we would expect to find the earliest plays lacking in this 'insider's look' quality, and for this aspect gradually to appear in the plays as the playwright became more familiar with court life. This is simply not the case. Shakespeare's expert depiction of a royal court is there from the beginning.

In fact, it would already be a stretch to say, as Stratfordians are obliged, that a player in the Lord Chamberlain's Men had a great deal of access to observe the court of Elizabeth I. Unlike the relatively privileged status they enjoyed as the King's Men under James, the Lord Chamberlain's Men were simply another one of the acting companies of London that Elizabeth enjoyed from time to time. They were not servants of the court and would not have been welcome to hang about there when not busy putting on a play. Even the much more privileged access granted to the company once they became the King's Men would not have been extended to such things as sitting in on Privy Council meetings, for example. Such limited exposure is clearly not a plausible explanation for the comprehensive, accurate portrayal of royal courts in Shakespeare's plays.

The History Plays as Succession Tract

Shakespeare's history plays are ten that dramatize a certain time period in English history and are all named for the king who was on the English throne during the period in which the play is set. All of the history plays except for *Henry VIII* were written during Elizabeth's reign. In fact, *Henry VIII* is one of the two, along with *King John*, that are stand-alone history plays. That is, the other eight all belong to one of two so-called tetralogies. Each tetralogy covers a single time period, more or less continuous, from the start of the first play to the end of the fourth and final play.

The first tetralogy that Shakespeare wrote, in the early 1590s, consists of the three *Henry VI* plays together with *Richard III*. These plays essentially cover the Wars of the Roses. Incidentally, the struggle gets the name 'Wars of the Roses' from the fact that each side used a different colour rose as one of its symbols – white for York and red for Lancaster. However, it didn't acquire this name until 1829, when Sir Walter Scot referred to the wars by this name in a book. He devised the name from a garden scene in *Henry VI, Part I*, where loyalty is displayed by the picking of either a red rose for Lancaster or a white rose for York. At the end of the last of the four plays, *Richard III*, the villainous Richard is defeated at the Battle of

Bosworth Field by the heroic Duke of Richmond, who is crowned King Henry VII. There is no mistaking who is the good guy and who is the bad guy in *Richard III*. Richard is thoroughly despicable, while Richmond is unambiguously noble. The message of the first tetralogy is clear: Henry VII was a heroic force for good who reunified England and brought peace to the land. Thus, the first tetralogy echoed and magnified James's message that positively highlighted his descent from Henry VII.

The second tetralogy begins with *Richard II*, which was written around 1595, the year after the publication of the Doleman tract. It continues with *Henry IV*, Parts I and II, culminating in *Henry V*, written in 1598. Although composed after the first tetralogy, the second tetralogy covers an earlier historical period – essentially the time immediately preceding the action of the first tetralogy. Amanda Mabillard demonstrated, in 'Representations of Kingship and Power in Shakespeare's Second Tetralogy', how the second tetralogy supports James's candidacy to succeed Elizabeth I:

> If we could find one reason for Shakespeare's second tetralogy containing the didactic message that a successful ruler must have divine authority, and first-rate political decision-making abilities which will ensure that England stays strong, (as Henry V could), it would have to be that the plays are intended, in part, as a guide to Elizabeth in choosing her heir. And, out of all the possible successors, only one seemed to come close to fitting the criteria outlined in the tetralogy – James VI of Scotland. (Mabillard, 2000a)

The First Folio classified plays into three categories: comedies, tragedies, and histories. The category of history plays only included the ten English histories named after English kings. It did not include, for example, *Julius Caesar, Coriolanus,* or *Antony and Cleopatra* – plays that could be classified as histories, Roman histories, anyway. *Coriolanus* and *Antony and Cleopatra* were written after James's accession to the English throne and are, therefore, not succession plays. *Julius Caesar*, on the other hand, was written just before the turn of the seventeenth century and can be considered the succession play *par excellence*. *Julius Caesar* portrays the chaos and civil war that ensues when the childless Caesar dies without having named a successor.

Small Latin and Less Greek

Ben Jonson famously wrote, in his poem 'To the Memory of My Beloved the Author, Mr. William Shakespeare and What He Hath Left Us', that he had 'small Latin and less Greek'. The quote has always been a bit of an embarrassment in terms of its exact meaning. The traditional explanation has tended to be that Jonson was straightforwardly acknowledging Shakespeare's lack of a classical education and his failure to master the Latin and Greek languages. The problem with this explanation, of course, is that the evidence from the works flatly contradicts such an explanation. That is, the works display an expert knowledge of both classical languages.

It is interesting to note that Jonson teased King James about his pronunciation of Latin. Jonson declared that 'his master G. Buchanan had corrupted his case when young and learned him to sing verses, when he should have read them'. James, for his part, disparaged English scholars' pronunciation of Latin, claiming: 'All the word knows that my master, Mr. George Buchanan, was a great master in that faculty [speaking

Latin]. I follow his pronunciation both of the Latin and Greek, and am sorry that my people of England do not the like; for certainly their pronunciation utterly spoils the grace of these two learned languages' (Stewart, 2011, p. 45).

Although there does seem to have been a genuine cultural difference in the way that the Scots and the English preferred Latin to be pronounced, Jonson's comments should not be mistaken for implying any sort of actual superiority on his part. James's mastery of Latin was beyond reproach, while Buchanan was widely considered one of Europe's greatest masters of the language. Remember that there were no native speakers of Latin around at the time to say what the correct pronunciation was – exactly how ancient Romans actually pronounced the language was and is a matter of scholarly best guesses. Jonson's comments are clearly meant in the manner of a good-natured joke. It's quite possible that the 'small Latin and less Greek' quip that the king's buddy wrote for the First Folio was a continuation of the joke.

'The play's the thing wherein I'll catch the conscience of the king'
—Hamlet (II.ii.604–605)

FOUR | **The Works**

I THOUGHT IT MIGHT BE FUN to consider the works of Shakespeare from the perspective that King James wrote them, confirmation bias be damned. I give no warrant with respect to how fully baked any of the following speculations may be. Nevertheless, I believe that some of them must be implied by his authorship, if he was the author.

It is notoriously hard to pin down exact composition dates for most of the plays; consequently, hardly any two chronologies of Shakespeare's works are identical. Candidates for the first extant play that he wrote, for instance, include: *Henry VI, Part I*; *Henry VI, Part II*; *The Comedy of Errors*; *The Two Gentlemen of Verona*; and *The Taming of the Shrew*.

Although not a great deal turns on precise dating, certain dates make better sense for certain plays than others, in a Jacobean context. For example, I believe that *The Taming of the Shrew*, which some scholars place somewhat earlier in the chronology, fits with the deterioration of James's relationship with Anna and therefore would have been written around 1593, rather than being one of his very first plays. Furthermore, the post-1592 dating of plays set in Italy or derived from Italian sources aligns with the fact that James didn't start receiving tutelage in Italian from Giacomo Castelvetro until then.

I provide here *Open Source Shakespeare*'s chronology of 37 plays, both in honour of what an invaluable resource it has been for this project and because this chronology maps so well onto important events in James's life; it even includes a play-less gap in 1603, the year taken up by the king's move from Edinburgh to London. Plays that have been chosen for further comment are in **bold**.

1589	**The Comedy of Errors**
1590	Henry VI, Part II
	Henry VI, Part III
1591	Henry VI, Part I
1592	**Richard III**
1593	**The Taming of the Shrew**
	Titus Andronicus
1594	**Romeo and Juliet**
	The Two Gentlemen of Verona
	Love's Labour's Lost
1595	**Richard II**
	A Midsummer Night's Dream
1596	King John
	Merchant of Venice
1597	Henry IV, Part I
	Henry IV, Part II
1598	Henry V
	Much Ado About Nothing
1599	Twelfth Night

	As You Like It
	Julius Caesar
1600	**Hamlet**
	The Merry Wives of Windsor
1601	Troilus and Cressida
1602	All's Well That Ends Well
1604	**Othello**
	Measure for Measure
1605	**King Lear**
	Macbeth
1606	Antony and Cleopatra
1607	Coriolanus
	Timon of Athens
1608	Pericles
1609	Cymbeline
1610	The Winter's Tale
1611	**The Tempest**
1612	Henry VIII

The Comedy of Errors

Around 1589, he wrote his first play, *The Comedy of Errors* – perhaps after meeting with the players that came to Edinburgh, perhaps before. A number of the play's characteristics set it apart from Shakespeare's other plays and suggest it may have been his first (or, at least, the earliest extant one). First of all, it is Shakespeare's shortest play, at approximately 14,700 words. The work is along the lines of a 'prentise' – something for the sake of practice and without any particular larger purpose. The fact that *The Comedy of Errors* is set in ancient Greece rather than the Italy of most of the 'Elizabethan' comedies is also consistent with James not yet having engaged Castelvetro's tutelage.

Henry VI

He then set out to write the first set of his kingship-propaganda history plays, the *Henry VI* trilogy. Becoming what is now known as part two of the group, the play displays the horrors of civil war and shows the dangers of a weak king, presenting the template for most of the history plays to follow: a monarch with a flaw that is detrimental to England. This flaw reflects favourably on James. Indeed, the flaws found in the kings of Shakespeare's history plays can be seen as advertisements for what the English would be avoiding by naming James as their sovereign. In other words, the kings in Shakespeare's plays serve as useful foils for their playwright-king.

Often, as in *Henry VI, Part II*, the flaw ultimately results in civil unrest. Presumably, James's intent was to scare the bejesus out of the gentry, in particular, who were easily frightened by tales of restless peasants. Another major purpose of the *Henry VI* plays is to provide the backdrop for *Richard III* and its happy ending, with its slaying of the villainous Richard by the soon-to-be-crowned Henry Tudor. Elements of the play that foreshadow events in *Richard III* strongly suggest that the playwright wrote the *Henry VI* plays with *Richard III* in mind.

Also present in this trilogy is another element common to the history plays: misogyny. Many of James's potential rival claimants to the English throne were women – Arabella Stuart, Anne Stanley, Isabella Clara Eugenia. The playwright guides the audience to think about the succession, English nationalism, and the throne at the same time that he's inserting a subtextual warning about the dangers of women and feminine power. Marjorie Garber has invited us to consider

> [*Henry VI, Part I*'s] models of English (male) heroism and dangerous French (female) opposition and perfidy. The

cross-dressed, martial Joan, who defeated both the French Dauphin ... and the English Talbot in single combat, is one such [dangerous woman] ...; the other is the seductively feminine Margaret of Anjou, the bride of Henry VI. ... [B]oth are presented as duplicitous threats to English power and manhood. (Garber, 2004, p. 91)

Richard III

Richard III introduces another 'bad king'. As a super-villain, Richard is not so much a foil for James (as it's not as if James could have accused Arabella Stuart or any of the other rivals for the throne of being a super-villain). Rather, Richard serves as the foil for the super-hero of the Shakespearean canon, the Duke of Richmond, who transforms in this play into Henry VII. There is little nuance to Richmond – he has none of the flaws that make other Shakespearean heroes so human. Notably, James would always compare himself favourably to Henry VII. James liked to remind Englishmen that he was descended 'from the loins' of Henry VII. As mentioned earlier, Henry VII was one of the three historical figures with whom James most frequently associated himself publicly.

The Taming of the Shrew

James then took a break from self-promotion for a while, writing some plays set in Italy and/or from Italian sources, drawing on his Italian lessons from Giacomo Castelvetro that he'd started early in the 1590s. The first of these, *The Taming of the Shrew*, deals with subject matter that was very close to home for the king. By 1593, relations between him and Anna had grown strained, and Anna was entertaining intrigues at court that were not always strictly aligned with the king's interests.

Historians hold differing opinions with respect to Anna, which range from dismissing her as frivolous to seeing her as a fairly significant asset and/or countervailing detriment to James's political objectives. Certainly, some characterize her as shrewish. D. H. Wilson, for example, stated: '[S]he had a quick temper. High words came easily and in her childish tantrums she could be violent, spiteful, indiscreet, and quite ingenious in her efforts to annoy. Hence the early years of the King's married life were far from tranquil' (Wilson, 1959, p. 95).

Perhaps *The Taming of the Shrew* was, in part, an expression of James's fantasy regarding his wife. In any event, in reality, Anne retained an independent streak for the rest of her life. At one point, as noted earlier, she even converted to Catholicism. This embarrassing fact was definitely kept on the down low, however, including by Anne herself.

Romeo and Juliet

James turned his attention in his next work, the first of his great tragedies, to the first and most profound love of his life: Esmé Stuart. To be perfectly clear: yes, I am suggesting that the greatest love story of all time, synonymous with love, especially in its 'young', 'at first sight', and 'true' forms, was actually based on the boy–man love of a thirteen-year-old prince and his thirty-seven-year-old cousin. As he had with 'Ane Metaphoricall Invention of a Tragedie Called Phoenix', James switched the gender of one of the lovers. The playwright also made Romeo the more socially acceptable age of seventeen.

The 'love at first sight' experienced by the two protagonists was not a figment of the playwright's imagination – after all,

James had experienced the phenomenon upon his introduction to Esmé in 1579. Indeed, all contemporary accounts report both the instantaneous nature of the young king's infatuation and its profound intensity.

It is commonplace to recognize that, in the play, the two ancient houses of Capulet and Montague, 'alike in honour and dignity', represent Catholicism and Protestantism. In real life, James, although baptized as a Catholic, had been raised a Protestant since his accession to the Scottish throne, while Esmé Stuart was a French Catholic who had converted to Protestantism in Scotland. Juliet's famous speech that begins with 'O Romeo, Romeo! Wherefore art thou Romeo? / Deny thy father and refuse thy name' (II.ii.33–36) can thus be translated as 'O Esmé, Esmé! Why are you Catholic? Deny your heritage and convert'. The Roman Catholicism is right there in the first name, isn't it? ROMEo.

Juliet continues, "'Tis but thy name that is my enemy. . . . What's in a name? That which we call a rose / By any other word would smell as sweet. . . . Romeo, doff thy name, / and for that name, which is no part of thee, / Take all myself' (II, ii, 38–49). Romeo replies, 'I take thee at thy word. / Call me but love, and I'll be new baptised. / Henceforth I never will be Romeo' (II, ii, 49–51). This exactly mirrors what happened in real life. Esmé converted to Protestantism and never recanted, even after returning to Catholic France.

Despite this conversion, the Protestant nobles remained suspicious of Esmé's true allegiance and, as we've seen, forced him into exile to France as a result of the Ruthven raid. In the play, Romeo is exiled by the Prince of Verona after he's killed Tybalt. In real life, the Protestant nobles forced Esmé into exile after he'd had the Earl of Morton executed. The play dramatizes the trauma associated with banishment and exile, a theme the playwright would explore in other plays, such as *Richard II*, *King Lear*, and *Coriolanus*.

Exile is explicitly linked with death in the play. In fact, Romeo considers exile a punishment worse than death. In Act III, Scene 3, when he learns from Friar Lawrence the punishment he is to receive for killing Tybalt, he exclaims, 'Ha, banishment! Be merciful, say "death," / For exile hath more terror in his look, / Much more than death. Do not say "banishment"' (III.iii.12–14). Encouraged by Friar Lawrence to look on the bright side – after all, 'the world is broad and wide' – Romeo retorts, 'There is no world with Verona walls / But purgatory, torture, hell itself. / Hence "banished" is banished from the world, / And world's exile is death. Then "banished" / Is death mistermed. Calling death "banishment," / Thou cut'st my head off with a golden ax and smilest upon the stroke that murders me' (III.iii.17–23).

Love's Labour's Lost

Love's Labour's Lost is set in Navarre, of all places. Navarre, remember, was the other short-listed kingdom in the running to supply the young James's royal bride. After lengthy negotiations, Navarre lost out to Denmark. It also happened to be the stomping ground of James's literary idol, Guillaume Saluste du Bartas.

Richard II

Around 1595, James wrote the first play in his next tetralogy: Richard II. Composed entirely in verse (even the common people speak in poetry – highly unusual for a Shakespeare play), it relates the downfall of Richard II and his replacement by his cousin Henry Bolingbroke, who is crowned Henry IV by play's end. The work is simultaneously a vigorous defence of the divine right of kings and a primer on the deposition of a monarch. We have already seen how *Richard II* was used by the conspirators in the failed Essex rebellion and noted that Queen Elizabeth had found its deposition scene so inflammatory that she had it officially removed from all copies of the play. There is a telling postscript regarding this infamous scene. In 1608, King James officially restored the deposition scene to *Richard II*, declaring that he had 'an affectionate remembrance of Essex' (Black, 1955, p. 374).

A Midsummer Night's Dream

He then dashed off *A Midsummer Night's Dream*, on the one hand an innocuous (although particularly ribald, even by Shakespearean standards), light comedy, while on the other hand a brilliant response to a play by Robert Greene called *The Scottish History of James the Fourth*. Greene's play includes a character named Oberon and uses the setting of James IV's court to criticize James VI's. In fact, Greene explicitly draws the connection: in the induction, a character by the name of Bohan exclaims, 'In the year 1520 was in Scotland a king, overruled with parasites, misled by lust, and many circumstances too long to trattle on now, much like our court of Scotland this day'.

The Merchant of Venice

The other play of 1596, the year that saw James put his finances in the hands of the Octavians, was *The Merchant of Venice*. This play is concerned with financial transactions, especially the rights of creditors and debtors.

By 1596, James would likely have been able to read the source material – *Il Pecorone* (*The Simpleton*), by Giovanni Fiorentino – in its original Italian, having had a few years of instruction from Castelvetro by that point; in 1596, *Il Pecorone* had not been translated into any other languages. Almost the whole plot of *The Merchant of Venice* is lifted from *Il Pecorone*. Fiorentino's original story concerns a debt, to a Jew, of a pound of flesh. The wife of the debtor's friend, by speaking of true justice, convinces the judge to rule against the Jew. *The Merchant of Venice* contains an additional sub-plot, concerning suitors for a potential bride having to win her by choosing the 'correct' casket out of three, made of either gold, silver, or lead. Shakespeare also made Shylock a usurer (i.e., he charged interest on the loan), which was not in the original story (Mabillard, 2000b). A more general source for the character of Shylock is the *commedia dell'arte* stock character 'Pantalone', the miserly old Venetian merchant who was a frequent villain in *commedia* plays.

Henry IV, Parts I and II

Perhaps King James devoted 1597 to cranking out the two parts of *Henry IV*, the plays that showcase the destructive fallout from the former Bolingbroke's usurpation of the divinely ordained Richard II. While Henry IV may be a more capable monarch than Richard II, Henry's reign is cursed by the 'sin' of usurping the divinely ordained Richard. His rule is constantly threatened by rebellion.

Although the plays are named for Henry IV, the real protagonist is his son Hal, who will become Henry V by the end of Part II. We watch as Henry IV's son transforms over the last three plays in the tetralogy from Hal, the wastrel associate of fun-loving rogues, to King Henry V, heroic victor at Agincourt. The plays are thus a demonstration of primogeniture 'working'. *Henry IV,* Parts I and II tell the tale of the eldest son of the reigning monarch. While Henry IV obtained his crown through usurpation, Hal obtained his through the strict application of primogeniture. The rebellion and woes that plague England in the *Henry IV* plays will be replaced by glorious victories in *Henry V*.

Henry V

The concluding play of the Henriad, *Henry V*, written around 1599, carries on the advert for a Jacobean succession. In Act 1, Scene 2, the Archbishop of Canterbury goes on for over sixty lines in an explication of something called 'Salic law'. Salic law had been developed by the Franks, the Germanic tribe that preceded and gave its name to France. Succession under Salic law strictly prohibited female inheritance. The Archbishop outlines to King Henry that Salic law doesn't apply to Henry's situation and that the law therefore supports an invasion of France to uphold a claim to the throne in a line descending from a female ancestor.

With this interpretation of Salic law in the audience's mind, King Henry brings up the danger of an invasion by the Scots should the English decide to invade France (which would necessitate taking troops out of England, leaving it vulnerable). Without explicitly saying it, the playwright leaves it up to the audience of the day to figure out the applicability of this historical scenario to the succession question. First of all, the play makes clear that Salic law does not apply in England, which was important for James's claim, dependent as it was on descent from his mother. In addition, by accepting James's claim to the English throne, the English would immediately solve their Scottish problem. With a union of the crowns, England wouldn't have to worry about Scots at its postern gate, so to speak.

To drive the point home, the play emphasizes that it is not only Englishmen in Henry's 'band of brothers' in France. Indeed, all four of the characters bearing the rank of captain hail from the other nations of the British Isles: Captain Macmorris is Irish, Captain Jamy is a Scot, and both Captain Gower and Captain Fluellen are Welsh. The unspoken message is: 'Don't you see what we can accomplish as a united island?' The follow-up message, as in all of Shakespeare's Elizabethan histories, is: 'All of this can be yours, England, with just one easy accession of James VI of Scotland to your throne'.

This multiculturalism makes *Henry V* the first of Shakespeare's 'British' plays, in a way – that is, plays advertising the idea of 'Great Britain', the nations of the British Isles united not just under the person of one king, as they would be by James's union of the crowns in 1603, but as one unitary country (which would not happen until the formation of the United Kingdom in 1707). Although the later plays *King Lear* and *Cymbeline* would be set in an earlier period, before the separate kingdoms of England, Scotland, and Wales were established, *Henry V* attempts to lay the groundwork for a program (ultimately unsuccessful) aiming to have Englishmen perceive themselves as British rather than just English.

James may have drawn inspiration for the famous scene on the eve of the battle of Agincourt (where Henry disguises himself as a private and mixes with his troops) from his maternal grandfather, James V. Legend has it that James V liked to disguise himself as a commoner and travel around Scotland, calling himself 'Gudeman of Ballengeich'. 'Gudeman' means farmer or landlord, while Ballengeich is Gaelic for 'windy pass', which was the nickname for a road near Stirling Castle. While many legends have been passed down that cast James V in a heroic light (using his Gudeman persona to catch out corrupt lairds and deliver their comeuppance, for example), it's quite likely the disguise and pseudonym were simply the cover James V used in the course of a royal hobby that produced at least nine illegitimate children, born to mothers drawn from all ranks of society.

Julius Caesar

After the string of rom-coms *Much Ado About Nothing*, *Twelfth Night*, and *As You Like It*, from which one might infer that James had abandoned his theatrical quest for the English throne, he came back with a vengeance in *Julius Caesar*. Simply put, the play is a cautionary tale depicting Rome's descent into civil war after its ruler dies without naming a successor. Likely written in the latter half of 1599, *Julius Caesar* is stridently yet craftily misogynistic, and the play has a paranoid, millennial air to it. It dwells on the inability of Caesar's wife, Calpurnia, to have children, directly analogous to the sixty-six-year-old Queen Elizabeth. The play's message was clear: to avoid chaotic and bloody civil war, England needed a (preferably male) successor lined up before Elizabeth died (i.e., ASAP). Given that some of the other front runners for the throne were women, particularly his perhaps greatest rival, Arabella Stuart, the implicit answer to the question that the play was meant to raise in the minds of the gentry was James – naming him as successor would avert catastrophe. *Julius Caesar* was written at a time when James's impatience to wear the English crown was starting to reach fever pitch.

Hamlet

We now turn to *the* play: *Hamlet*. It is widely acknowledged to be the most autobiographical of Shakespeare's plays. That is, commentators are consistently drawn to the conclusion that we're not just experiencing Shakespeare's usual mastery of incarnating his characters – there has to be a good deal of the playwright himself in the Prince of Denmark. Paradoxically, this experience is often accompanied by a feeling, first expressed by Samuel Taylor Coleridge, that we as readers or playgoers 'have a smack of Hamlet' ourselves.

The Tragedy of Hamlet, Prince of Denmark was entered into the Stationers' Register in 1602 – the year before Elizabeth I died and James ascended the English throne. At this point, Robert Cecil had already decided that James should become the king after Elizabeth's death and was secretly arranging for as smooth a transition to that eventuality as possible. Incidentally, the name is derived from the source, the story of *Amleth*, in a chronicle of Danish history by the twelfth-century writer Saxo Grammaticus (the 'H' has simply been moved from the end of the name to the beginning); its similarity to the name of Shakspere's son Hamnet is purely coincidental (irrespective of the playwright's identity).

It's worth reviewing the plot of *Hamlet* in some detail. At midnight, atop the battlements of Elsinore Castle, a sentry is in the middle of telling Prince Hamlet's friend Horatio that a ghost resembling Hamlet's recently deceased father had appeared the previous night, 'when yond same star that's westward from the pole / Had made his course t'illume that part of heaven / Where now it burns' (I.i.34–37). Suddenly the same ghost appears, doesn't reply to Horatio's attempt to engage it in conversation, and disappears again.

In between the death of Hamlet's father and the start of the play, Hamlet's uncle, Claudius, had married Hamlet's mother, Gertrude, and been elected king (that is, pursuant to the elective monarchy in place in Denmark at the time, he was chosen to be the new king by a consensus of the powerful Danish nobles). Hamlet is distrustful of Claudius, suspecting what he would later prove, that '[h]e that hath killed my king, and whored my mother / Popped in between th'election and my hopes' (V.ii.69). Hamlet had hoped to succeed his father, but while it was common under elective monarchy for an elder son to be elected king after his father's death, it was by no means certain.

Claudius dispatches two ambassadors to speak to the aged King of Norway to inform him of the actions of the Norwegian king's rogue nephew, Fortinbras, who is preparing to invade Denmark. The events of the Danish succession have led Fortinbras to suspect instability and therefore weakness in the Danish state, and he has begun sabre rattling – demanding that Denmark give back lands that his father had lost to Hamlet's.

We are introduced to the Secretary of State, Polonius, and his family. Polonius gives fatherly advice to his son, Laertes, who is heading off to study in France. Polonius's daughter, Ophelia, is Hamlet's girlfriend.

The ghost appears to Hamlet and tells him that Claudius did, indeed, murder him by putting poison in his ear while he slept in his orchard. Rather than simply taking the word of a ghost, who might be an evil spirit trying to trick him, Hamlet decides he needs further evidence before exacting revenge upon Claudius. In the meantime, the ambassadors report back from Norway that the Norwegians' intentions are not to invade Denmark but to conquer an insignificant piece of land in

Poland that they would like to get to by moving their troops through Denmark.

A group of travelling players (i.e., an acting troupe) from the city arrives at Elsinore. Hamlet greets them warmly and familiarly, commenting on how one actor has grown a beard since he last saw him and how much the boy-actor[5] has grown. Hamlet decides to use the actors to 'catch the conscience of the king' by having them perform a play, *The Murder of Gonzago*, that re-enacts the murder of his father according to what the ghost told him. If Claudius reacts suspiciously to the play, the prince will have confirmation of the ghost's claim to be the spirit of his murdered father. Shortly thereafter, Hamlet delivers the world's undisputed all-time champion speech of speeches, the soliloquy that opens with, 'To be, or not to be'.

The actors perform the play, wherein a king's brother poisons the king, marries the king's queen, and becomes king himself. Claudius is visibly upset and leaves. He subsequently informs us via soliloquy that he is, indeed, guilty of his brother's murder.

Hamlet visits his mother in her chamber, where Polonius has hidden himself behind drapes. Hamlet is openly hostile toward Gertrude, who cries, 'Thou wilt not murder me?', making Polonius gasp. Hamlet, believing the hidden Polonius to be Claudius, stabs the old man through the drapes, killing him. Claudius sends Hamlet away on a ship to England with Rosencrantz and Guildenstern, whom he has previously instructed to accompany the prince.

Laertes returns from France, angry and confused about his father's death. Horatio receives a letter from Hamlet informing

---

5. Boy-actors would play the women's parts, since women were not allowed on stage in this era.

him that the prince switched a letter Claudius had sent with Rosencrantz and Guildenstern, requesting that the King of England kill Hamlet; instead, the letter requests Rosencrantz's and Guildenstern's executions. Claudius also receives a letter from Hamlet indicating he is returning to Denmark. Claudius and Laertes scheme to murder Hamlet by having Laertes challenge the prince to a duel, wherein the tip of Laertes's sword will be coated in poison, and poison will be added to Hamlet's drink. Meanwhile, Ophelia has drowned in a river, apparently having committed suicide.

Hamlet and Horatio speak with a gravedigger, who informs them that one of the skulls lying around belonged to a court jester, named Yorick, with whom Hamlet was once rather familiar. Laertes appears and jumps into Ophelia's grave, then he and Hamlet tussle. Soon after, Osric, a dandy for whom Hamlet has nothing but contempt, informs the prince that the king would like Laertes and Hamlet to have a friendly duel.

A bloodbath ensues. Queen Gertrude drinks from the poisoned cup. Hamlet gets scratched by the poison-tipped sword, then Hamlet and Laertes switch swords, after which Laertes is scratched by the poison-tipped sword. Gertrude dies from the poison. Hamlet then forces Claudius to drink from the same cup, whereupon the king dies. Laertes dies from his poisoned wound. Hamlet, as he is dying, asks Horatio to 'report me and my cause aright / To the unsatisfied'. Horatio replies, 'I am more an antique Roman than a Dane' (V.ii.337), wishing instead to die with his dearest friend. Hamlet insists otherwise, then tells Horatio that he thinks Fortinbras, who has just arrived from Poland, should become the next king of Denmark. Fortinbras enters with the English ambassadors, who deliver the news that Rosencrantz and Guildenstern are dead. Fortinbras then announces his intention to claim the throne, saying, 'I have some rights of memory in this kingdom / Which now to claim my vantage doth invite me' (V.ii.390–391).

The Autobiographical Interpretation
I think Simon Schama was spot on when he referred to *Hamlet* as a reflection of James's life. It is a reflection not just of the king's early life but also of contemporary events regarding his efforts to succeed Elizabeth to the English throne, with James placing himself in the title role.

We orient ourselves by identifying Gertrude as Mary, Queen of Scots. Mary's first husband, King Francis II, had died of a mysterious ear condition, and some believed he had been murdered, while her second husband, Henry Darnley (James's father) had been killed in an orchard. Shortly after Darnley's murder, Mary wedded one of his suspected killers, James Hepburn, the 4th Earl of Bothwell. Gertrude, as the widow of a king killed in an orchard by drops of poison in the ear, and as the newlywed bride of her slain husband's suspected murder, clearly represents Mary, Queen of Scots. That makes Hamlet, as Gertrude's son (and the son of a man killed in an orchard), representative of James.

Once Hamlet is identified as James, however, the characters of Claudius and the Ghost of Hamlet's father can be seen to represent different people when looked at in relation to James. Claudius is Elizabeth I, and the Ghost is Mary, Queen of Scots. As Claudius is the killer of Hamlet's parent, Elizabeth was the killer of James's parent. This identification of Claudius as James's cousin Elizabeth is strengthened by the fact that Claudius refers to Hamlet four times as 'cousin' (the play's only use of the word) but never as 'nephew' (George Mason University, 2015). The identification of the Ghost as the Catholic Mary is strengthened by the fact that the Ghost seems to be in purgatory, a Catholic category of the afterlife. While Hamlet is compelled by honour to avenge his father, the play suggests that his father had done some wicked things in his lifetime, paralleling James's view of his mother. With this interpretation, Hamlet's (mostly internal) struggle to replace Claudius as monarch of Denmark becomes a reflection of James's struggle to replace Elizabeth as monarch of England.

As noted earlier, Elizabeth's Secretary of State was William Cecil until his death in 1598. Many people, over the years, have recognized William Cecil in the character of Polonius. One of the pieces of evidence for this recognition is a letter the elder Cecil wrote to his son Robert, containing what he called 'certain precepts for the well ordering of man's life', that bears a striking resemblance to Polonius's famous advice to his son Laertes before he goes off to school in France. For instance, William advises Robert to 'beware of suretyship for thy best friend, for he which payeth another man's debts seeks his own decay', and 'neither borrow money of a neighbour or friend but rather from a stranger, where paying for it thou mayest hear no more of it, for otherwise thou shalt eclipse thy credit, lose thy freedom, and yet pay to him as dear as to the other'. This compares to Polonius's advice to 'neither a borrower nor a lender be, for loan oft loses both itself and friend' (Roth, 2015).

If Polonius represents William Cecil, then Laertes represents Robert. Both Laertes and Robert attended university in France (the latter at the Sorbonne). In real life, James had despised William Cecil but had, around the time of the writing of *Hamlet*, been able to join in common cause with Robert Cecil. This parallels Hamlet's relationship with Laertes. In Act V, Scene 2, Hamlet remarks, 'But I am very sorry, good Horatio, / That to Laertes I forgot myself, / For by the image of my cause I see / The portraiture of his. I'll court his favours. / But sure the bravery of his grief did put me / Into a towering passion' (V.ii.80–85).

The pair of diplomats Rosencrantz and Guildenstern parallel the pair of diplomats John Erskine, Earl of Mar, and Edward Bruce, Lord Kinloss, who were sent to negotiate, first with the Earl of Essex and, after the failure of the rebellion, with Robert Cecil. Rosencrantz and Guildenstern were childhood schoolmates of Hamlet, just as the Earl of Mar had been a childhood schoolmate of James. In the play, Hamlet is able to change the instructions to the King of England. In real life, James was able to change the instructions of Erskine and Bruce before his instructions aligned James with the doomed Essex rebellion.

Fortinbras represents Philip III of Spain. Both Fortinbras and Philip have the same name as their respective fathers (i.e., Philip III's father was Philip II, and while the play doesn't specify what number Fortinbras is, it must be at least 'II'). At the end of the play, Fortinbras arrives with his army to claim the throne. The instability in Denmark, a direct result of uncertainty regarding the succession, has prompted Fortinbras to move in and around Denmark with his army, as if he were stalking prey, looking for the right time to strike and arriving at Elsinore at the most convenient moment to seize the throne. The implicit message of *Hamlet* is that elective monarchy is unstable. In this respect, *Hamlet* can be seen as another of Shakespeare's succession plays, one more advert warning of the dangers of any system of monarchical succession that didn't adhere to primogeniture. It's not just the virtues of certainty produced by strict adherence to primogeniture that *Hamlet* demonstrates; under the rules of primogeniture, the whole incentive for Claudius to kill his brother disappears – the death of the elder Hamlet would not create an opportunity for Claudius, since the throne would automatically pass to Prince Hamlet.

It is also worth noting that *Hamlet* contains plenty of that other hallmark of a Shakespearean succession play: misogyny (e.g., 'Frailty, thy name is woman!'). The portrayal of Gertrude is not particularly positive. The parallels between Gertrude and Mary, Queen of Scots are obvious. Where was the all of the outrage that James displayed at *The Faerie Queene*'s portrayal of Duessa? Why did James not call for the arrest and punishment of Shakespeare, as he had with Spenser?

For a more through-the-looking-glass flavour to this interpretation, consider the possibility that James was using *Hamlet* to carry on the coded correspondence with Cecil regarding the succession. Recall that each of the important players were given code numbers and that King James was assigned the number thirty. In order for this secret code interpretation to have any merit, we would therefore expect to find the character Hamlet identified by the number thirty. Lo and behold, the character of Hamlet is indirectly, but quite clearly, identified as being thirty years old by the gravedigger. Hamlet and the gravedigger, who is unaware that he is speaking to the prince, have the following exchange (V.i.122–127):

> HAMLET. How long hast thou been grave-maker?
>
> GRAVEDIGGER. Of all the days i'th'year I came to't that day that our last king Hamlet overcame Fortinbras.
>
> HAMLET. How long is that since?
>
> GRAVEDIGGER. Cannot you tell that? Every fool can tell that. It was that very day that young Hamlet was born: he that is mad and sent into England.

A few lines later, the gravedigger, referring to himself as a 'sexton' (a person responsible for maintaining a church's graveyard), declares, 'I have been sexton here man and boy thirty years' (V.i.139–140). The gravedigger started on the day of Hamlet's birth, and he has been a sexton for thirty years; therefore, Hamlet is thirty.

The Cosmological Interpretation

Amazingly, there is another mind-boggling Jacobean interpretation of *Hamlet* alongside the autobiographical one. It would seem that with *Hamlet*, James harkened back to his meeting with Tycho Brahe and their learned discussion about Copernican theory. This interpretation draws on the work of Peter Usher. In *Shakespeare and the Dawn of Modern Science*, Usher, a retired astrophysicist, posited evidence of Shakespeare's attention to early modern astronomy in five plays – *Love's Labour's Lost, Hamlet, Cymbeline, The Merchant of Venice*, and *The Winter's Tale* (Usher, 2010). With respect to *Hamlet*, Usher has provided evidence that the play depicts the battle for the hearts and minds of European astronomers that was going on in Shakespeare's day. Usher's remarkable insight was that the characters in *Hamlet* represent important figures in the development of the 'New Astronomy' taking hold in the sixteenth and early seventeenth centuries. The most significant difference between Usher's cosmological interpretation and mine is that while Usher identifies Tycho Brahe with Rosencrantz and Guildenstern, I think Brahe is better identified with Hamlet. Thus, the following borrows Usher's premise, his identification of Claudius with Ptolemy and of Fortinbras with Copernicus, and his interpretation of some of the text. The rest falls on me.

We begin with the premise that in the play, the status of King of Denmark represents the status of the cosmological model that was generally accepted by European astronomers in the latter half of the sixteenth century. That is, the character who wears the crown indicates which model is preeminent. At the start of the play, Claudius is the king. Claudius represents Claudius Ptolemy, the second-century Egyptian mathematician and astronomer presented earlier in this book. Egypt was, in Ptolemy's time, a Roman province. Ptolemy's *Almagest* was an astronomical treatise that contained a geocentric model of the cosmos. This Ptolemaic model was (almost) universally accepted by educated Europeans from Ptolemy's time up until the 1543 publication of Copernicus's *De revolutionibus orbium coelestium* (*On the Revolution of the Heavenly Spheres*). Acceptance of the heliocentric model did not happen immediately, mind you, but gradually became accepted as its advantages over the geocentric model became increasingly apparent to astronomers.

De revolutionibus was written by Nicolaus Copernicus, a Polish astronomer. As I've already indicated, Copernicus is represented in *Hamlet* by Fortinbras, who comes from Poland to claim the throne at the play's end. This represents the fact that Copernican theory was supplanting Ptolemaic theory in Europe at the turn of the seventeenth century.

The action of the play represents the failed attempt by Brahe (Hamlet) to have his geoheliocentrism become the preeminent cosmological model. In the process, both Hamlet/geoheliocentrism and Claudius/geocentrism die, leaving Fortinbras/heliocentrism to claim the throne.

We've had the idea, since Russell Doescher, Don Olson, and Marilynn Olson first made the identification in 1998, that when Bernardo refers to 'the star that's westward from the pole', he is describing Tycho's star, the supernova of 1572 ("SN 1572," n.d.). Just as, in Brahe's eyes, the appearance of this new star had been another strike against the cosmology of Ptolemy's *Almagest*, the ghost of Hamlet's father seems to confirm what Hamlet has suspected about Claudius. Rather than taking the encounter with the ghost as absolute proof of his uncle's guilt, he sets up an experiment (using the travelling players' performance of *The Murder of Gonzago*) to test the theory. This is consistent with Brahe's systematic scrutiny of the heavens; he became one of the first modern scientists by testing theory with careful, methodical observations of nature. Only after the results of the test have corroborated the ghost's story, and Hamlet has checked his own observations against Horatio's (which support the prince's), is Hamlet convinced that he should kill Claudius. In real life, careful observation and measurement of the heavens convinced Brahe that there were too many problems with Ptolemy's geocentric model. Since he wasn't prepared to accept Copernican heliocentrism, he came up with his own Tychonic, geoheliocentric model.

The report by the English ambassador that 'Rosencrantz and Guildenstern are dead' represents the material change that Thomas Digges made to the 1576 edition of *A Prognostication Everlasting*, a book of astronomical facts, which also contained a perpetual calendar, first published by Thomas's father, Leonard Digges. While editions of the elder Digges's work had adhered strictly to the Ptolemaic model, Thomas's 1576 edition contained a detailed discussion of the Copernican model. It was the first English publication of the heliocentric model and contained the first translations into English of *De revolutionibus*. The agents of Claudius are dead. The English ambassadors enter the stage simultaneously with Fortinbras, just in time to recognize his claim to the throne.

The character of Horatio, whose named is derived from that of the Greek playwright Horace, represents the playwright, James. When Horatio tells Hamlet, 'I am more an antique Roman than a Dane', this is James declaring himself in favour of Ptolemaic geocentrism, rather than the Tychonic model (or the Copernican one, for that matter). Ptolemy had lived in the Roman Empire and was, therefore, an ancient ('antique') Roman.

The character of Osric, in terms of the cosmological interpretation, represents an academic named Andreas Osiander. The foppish Osric cares only for appearance, not reality or the truth. Hamlet, toying with him, gets him to agree first that it's cold, then that it's actually hot. Osric's deplorable disregard for the truth mirrors Osiander's unseemly 'contribution' to the Copernican revolution. Osiander, shocked that the Copernican system claimed, in contradiction to scripture, to be true (rather than simply mathematically useful), urged Copernicus to include a statement to the effect that even if the Copernican system did result in correct astronomical computations, it may not be true. Despite the fact that Copernicus flatly refused to include such a statement, Osiander – who had been entrusted with the printing of *De revolutionibus* – took advantage of the fact that Copernicus lay dying in Poland; Osiander inserted his own preface, unsigned and therefore implied to be from Copernicus, asserting the former's 'fictionalist' interpretation of the treatise ("Osiander, Andreas," 2008). Hamlet's open contempt for Osric, I speculate, reflects Brahe's contempt for Osiander, which I suggest he revealed in the conversation about Copernican theory that James and Brahe engaged in on that momentous day in March 1590.

The Phoenix and the Turtle

In 1601, *Love's Martyr*, a long poem by an obscure poet named Robert Chester, was published along with shorter poetry written by much bigger names, such as Ben Jonson, George Chapman, and William Shakespeare. Printed by Richard Field, the poems were all variations on the story of the love between the phoenix and the turtledove. Shakespeare's entry, originally published without a title but conventionally referred to as *The Phoenix and the Turtle*, was an enigmatic allegory depicting various birds gathered for the funeral of the phoenix. People have been trying, and failing, to make proper sense of the poem ever since.

However, it actually seems to make sense if one assumes that James wrote it, as he had 'Ane Metaphoricall Invention of a Tragedie Called Phoenix', with Esmé Stuart in mind. The poem describes, in lines 25 to 31, the love between the turtle (King James) and his queen:

> So they lov'd, as love in twain
> Had the essence but in one;
> Two distincts, division none:
> Number there in love was slain.
>
> Hearts remote, yet not asunder,
> Distance, and no space was seen
> 'Twixt the turtle and his queen;

The poem concludes with a threnody, or funeral lament, reminiscent of the chest full of burned letters from Esmé:

> Here enclos'd in cinders lie.
> Death is now the phoenix's nest,
> And the turtle's loyal breast
> To eternity doth rest,
> Leaving no posterity—
> 'Twas not their infirmity,
> It was married chastity.

The fact that James and Esmé left no children behind was due not to any infirmity but to the lack of a uterus between them.

Othello

The first play James wrote when he was King of England was quite possibly *Othello*. The action takes place during the events that led to the Battle of Lepanto, when the Ottomans were making the opening moves in a campaign that would result in the eventual capture of the Venetian colonies on Cyprus. Thus, the setting of King James's poem *Lepanto* fits precisely in between *Othello*, which ends before the Battle of Lepanto, and *Much Ado About Nothing*, which starts shortly after that battle. Based on Cinthio's *Un Capitano Moro* (*A Moorish Captain*), *Othello* was another play drawn from a source for which there was, at the time, no English translation.

While quite a number of Shakespeare's plays contain themes of cuckoldry and male sexual jealousy (as did the plays of many other early modern playwrights), *Othello* was the playwright's major meditation upon this destructive facet of humanity. The play's villain, Iago, a master manipulator, is able to convince his commanding officer, Othello, that Othello's wife, Desdemona, has been unfaithful. By the play's end, Iago's machinations have stoked Othello's jealousy to such an extent that Othello murders Desdemona.

Although James himself didn't seem to suffer from excessive jealousy, it had certainly had a major impact upon his life. His father's murder of David Rizzio was a direct result of Darnley's sexual jealousy amidst the rumours of Rizzio's paternity – rumours that dogged James for most of his life (in Scotland, at any rate); only a few years prior to the writing of *Othello*, a

Scottish mob had been able to taunt him as the 'son of Seigneur Davy'. It's interesting that the existence of James himself, as an innocent, unborn baby, was the catalyst for the tragic murder of David Rizzio. Notably, Iago is the Spanish form of James. The centuries have seen much speculation about Iago's refusal to fully explain his motives for engineering this tragedy. Samuel Taylor Coleridge famously referred to Iago's 'motiveless malignity'. There is a parallel between the foetal James and Iago – both caused a jealous murder. Foetal James literally had no motive, of course, while Iago won't confess his.

Measure for Measure

Measure for Measure was probably written in 1604, right around the time that James was dealing with the Puritans at the Hampton Court Conference. With its title derived from the Sermon on the Mount (the only Shakespeare play to take its name from a biblical passage) and its themes of morality, sin, and judgement, *Measure for Measure* clearly reflects this timing. In his dealings with the Puritans, James must have been reminded again and again of the message of Mathew 7:1–5:

> 7.1 Judge not, that ye be not judged.
> 7.2 For with what judgment ye judge, ye shall be judged: and with what measure ye mete, it shall be measured to you again.
> 7.3 And why beholdest thou the mote that is in thy brother's eye, but considerest not the beam that is in thine own eye?
> 7.4 Or how wilt thou say to thy brother, Let me pull out the mote out of thine eye; and, behold, a beam is in thine own eye?

7.5 Thou hypocrite, first cast out the beam out of thine own eye; and then shalt thou see clearly to cast out the mote out of thy brother's eye.

The play's villain, Angelo, is rigid, judgemental, puritanical, and incapable of mercy. At the same time, he is every bit the hypocrite with a beam in his eye looking to cast out the mote in his brother's. At the start of the play the Duke of Vienna, pretending to leave Vienna but secretly staying disguised as a friar, puts Angelo in charge of the city. Angelo wastes no time in sentencing a character named Claudio to death for extramarital sex (Claudio has impregnated his own fiancée). When Claudio's sister, the nun-in-training Isabella, goes to plead for Claudio's life, Angelo suggests he will spare her brother's life in return for sexual favours.

The character of Vincentio, the Duke of Vienna, referred to in the play as 'the old fantastical duke of dark corners', is commonly seen as a representation of King James. Given his well-deserved reputation as one of the world's most secretive monarchs, the comparison is apt. It is not only James with whom the duke of dark corners is compared; Marjorie Garber noted: 'As often as this Duke has been compared to King James, he has also been compared to Shakespeare, or to a playwright, ordering his cast and bringing about his plot devices, dramatic surprises, and denouements' (Garber, 2004, p. 564).

King Lear

Surprised by the hostile reception to his project to form 'Great Britain' by parliamentary statute, James wrote *King Lear*. Simply put, *King Lear*, arguably his bleakest tragedy, is an artistic representation of the tragic consequences faced by a king of Britain when he decides to divide his kingdom into three. Lear has no sons, but he has three daughters: Goneril, Regan, and Cordelia. Goneril and Regan are married to the Dukes of Albany and Cornwall, respectively, while Cordelia is, as yet, unmarried. Considering the facts that 'Albany' is an archaic term for Scotland, while Cornwall was Celtic and in the southwest, *King Lear* represents the division of the mythically united Britain into England, Scotland, and Wales. At the start of the play, Lear plans to retire and transfer ownership of Scotland to Goneril, Wales and Cornwall to Regan, and England to Cordelia. However, he decides against giving Cordelia any territory after getting into a huff over a perceived insult and instead divides England between the other two daughters. Tragedy ensues. Held up to the mirror of *King Lear*, King James's plan to form Great Britain becomes simply a laudable goal to restore the *status quo ante*, before all of the tragedy that results from a disunited kingdom. *King Lear* was the first of two Shakespeare plays set in ancient Britain and supporting British unity; he would return to this setting in *Cymbeline*.

Macbeth

James had first-hand knowledge about ambition. After he had spent over a decade in single-minded pursuit of the English throne, its shine had already begun to wear off by 1605. *Shakespeare in Scotland* notes a number of connections that Shakespeare's plays have with Scotland. Among the more interesting connections with respect to *Macbeth* are a couple of instances where Shakespeare displays highly detailed knowledge of Scotland. Firstly, he accurately depicts an obscure point of Scottish royal protocol that is not found in the historical sources used for the play:

> In Act V, Macbeth gets ready for battle and calls out impatiently for his armor-bearer, named Seton. The legends of Macbeth do not mention any Setons, but adding him to the play was perfectly appropriate. Professor Wilson of the University of Edinburgh marveled that 'somehow or other' Shakespeare learned that the Setons were the hereditary armor-bearers to the kings of Scotland. (Maley & Murphy, 2004, p. xlii)

Secondly, he displays a remarkably accurate knowledge of the mysterious and (at the time) little-known geography of Scotland:

> Arthur Clark says Shakespeare correctly situates Dunsinane, Great Birnham Wood, Forres, Inverness, the Western Isles, Colmekill, Saint Colme, and the lands that gave their names to the thanes: Fife, Glamis, Cawdor, Ross, Lennox, Mentieth, Angus and Caithness. Maps of Scotland were rare, and only someone who had been there could have situated the places so accurately. Even the Scots were vague about their geography. (Maley & Murphy, 2004, p. 65)

The Tempest

In *The Tempest*, James returned once again to his meeting with Tycho Brahe. Had it not been for the North Sea tempest that had turned his fiancée's ships back on their trip from Denmark to Scotland, James would never have met the colourful astronomer and alchemist. It's not hard to see the resemblance between Brahe and the play's powerful protagonist, Prospero. Both men live on an island that they rule and upon which they wield a powerful book – one that gives its owner some measure of power over nature. In James's three poems about Brahe, he mentions the astronomer's book in two. In the last two lines of the first sonnet,

> Then greate is Ticho who by this his booke (Then great is
>   Tycho who by this his book)
> Commandement doth ouer these commanders brooke.
>   (Allows commandment over these commanders)

James clearly suggests that the book gives Brahe power over nature – i.e., supernatural power. In *The Tempest*, Prospero's book also gives him supernatural powers. The importance of the book to Prospero's power is underscored at the end of the play, when Prospero renounces magic and declares: 'deeper than did ever plummet sound / I'll drown my book' (V.i.56–57).

Time's glory is to calm contending kings,
To unmask falsehood and bring truth to light.
—*The Rape of Lucrece,* William Shakespeare

FIVE | **Conclusion**

How close is the match between what we know of King James and what the works of Shakespeare tell us about their author? Look at the following list of descriptors; can you tell whether the list, in its entirety, describes James or whether it describes Shakespeare, as evidenced by the biography of James and by the works of Shakespeare, respectively?

- The product of a superlative classical education
- A lyric poet, particularly fond of the sonnet form
- Witty with a bawdy sense of humour
- A lover of weddings
- Homosexual
- Misogynist but with a healthy respect for female sexuality
- Lame (lower limb disability)
- A close student of human motivation

- Fluent in English, Scots, Latin, Greek, French, Spanish, and Italian
- Familiar with witchcraft, astronomy, medicine, and law
- Fascinated by animals and the supernatural
- Obsessed with literature, hunting, the English crown, and the procreative habits of handsome young men
- Preoccupied with honour
- Anti-war
- Religiously tolerant but disdainful of puritans
- Champion of Henry VII, the divine right of kings, and a united 'Great Britain'
- Staunch upholder of rank, degree, hierarchy, and the status quo

If you answered 'both', then you fell for my little trap. The list actually describes James only. Although there is evidence of Shakespeare's intimate knowledge of Scotland and Scots culture, the works of Shakespeare do not display evidence of fluency (or the lack thereof) in the Scots language. Other than that one detail, however, the list is equally applicable to James Stuart and to the author of the works of Shakespeare. James fits the Shakespearean profile remarkably well.

Incorporating his identity as Shakespeare into James's life story would read something along the lines of the following. A young, sensitive boy-king with weak legs and a huge capacity for learning is given a world-class education. By about the age of thirteen he has fallen in love with the three passions that will, in one form or another, stay with him for life: language/literature, hunting, and his cousin, Esmé Stuart.

He gathers about him a Castalian Band of writers, poets, and musicians. In this environment, he develops and refines his craft. He publishes *The Essays of a Prentise, in the Divine Art of Poesie* in 1585. *Essays of a Prentise* contains his first tribute to the memory of Esmé, 'Ane Metaphoricall Invention of a Tragedie Called Phoenix'.

He sets his sights on succeeding Elizabeth I to the English throne, particularly after his mother is executed, in 1587. He writes a masque for a wedding in 1588. In 1589, a tempest causes him to sail to Denmark, where he marries Anna, stays at Elsinore Castle, and has a memorable meeting with Tycho Brahe on his island of Hven. Also in 1589, he meets with players travelling up from London, including the mysterious Lawrence Fletcher, who will be the first name listed in the royal patent creating the King's Men from the Lord Chamberlain's Men. Also in 1589, James writes his first play.

He hires Giacomo Castelvetro to teach him Italian in 1592, exposing him to the rich theatrical tradition of Italy and enabling him to discover and read, directly from the original, so many of the sources he would use in his career as a playwright. In 1593, Thomas Vautrolier's former apprentice, Richard Field, prints King James' poem *Venus and Adonis,* using the name William Shakespeare, remarkably similar to Field's Stratford neighbour, William Shakspere. *Venus and Adonis* makes William Shakespeare a name in the English poetry scene. In 1594, James writes his second tribute to the memory of Esmé Stuart, *Romeo and Juliet.* During the course of the 1590s, James writes at least a dozen propaganda works to bolster his succession campaign. These include ten plays: the three parts of *Henry VI, Richard III, Richard II, King John,* the two parts of *Henry IV, Henry V,* and *Julius Caesar.* His campaign also includes two prose works, *Basilikon Doron* and *The True Law of*

Free Monarchies.⁶ These works espouse a consistent point of view with respect to monarchy – that is, one based on male primogeniture and the divine right of kings. They are all consistent with James's claim to the throne. In 1601, Richard Field prints James's third tribute to the memory of Esmé Stuart, known as *The Phoenix and the Turtle*.

Although initially backing the wrong side, James emerges from the aftermath of the Essex Rebellion in a secret alliance with Robert Cecil to place him on the throne after Elizabeth's death. In 1602, the Stationers' Register notes his *Hamlet*, which contains elements suspiciously similar to those regarding the succession. He is crowned King of England in 1603. He writes *Measure for Measure* in response to his dealings with Puritans during the Hampton Court Conference. He writes two plays set in ancient Britain, *King Lear* and *Cymbeline*, in support of his project to legally unite England and Scotland. He begins to write *Henry VIII* in 1612 until grief over the death of his son Henry, and the weight of government in the wake of the death of Robert Cecil, cause him to employ another playwright, believed to be John Fletcher, to complete the work. He writes no more plays. In 1623, with James suffering from dementia, the *First Folio* is published. James dies in 1625.

Although it may take some time to get used to the idea that James was the identity behind the Shakespeare pseudonym, the theory is coherent and helps to explain many of the mysteries surrounding the Shakespeare Authorship Question. That James was the author is consistent with what we know about Shakespeare, including the criteria laid out by J. Thomas Looney in

---

6. That's without including *A Midsummer Night's Dream*, *Hamlet*, and *Daemonologie*, each of which presents a case for inclusion amongst the 'succession tracts'.

Shakespeare Identified. It's consistent with the way King James used his finely honed writing skills to bolster his authority and further his interests. It suggests that one of the reasons humanity has consistently found Shakespeare's exploration of kingship (and power more generally) to be irresistibly fascinating is because it was written from an insider's perspective.

I think the idea of James VI and I as the man behind the pseudonym is exciting. After all, real-life examples of a philosopher-king are rare enough. A playwright-king is a most rare thing, indeed – helped onto the English throne by his own plays, no less. Perhaps we've been underrating the genius of Shakespeare all along. . . .

APPENDIX 1

Three Sonnets Dedicated to Tycho Brahe

A Sonnet on Ticho Brahe

That onlie essence who made all of noght (That only
    essence who made all of nothing)
Our great and mightie Lord the life of all (Our great and
    mighty Lord the life of all)
When he in ordour euerie thing hade broght (When he in
    order everything had brought)
At the creating of this earthlie ball (At the creating of this
    earthly ball)
Then made he man at last. Thy raigne it shall (Then he
    made man at last. Thy reign it shall)
Extend (quod Jehoua) in euerie cace (Extend [said Jehova] in
    every case)
Ouer all these breathing beasts that flatlie fall (Over all
    these breathing beasts that flatly fall)
For humble homage here before thy face (For humble
    homage here before your face)

He also pitch'd eache Planet in his place (He also put each
   planet in its place)
And made them rulers of the ruling Lord (And made them
   rulers of the ruling Lord)
As heauenlie impes to gouerne bodies basse (As heavenly
   spirits to govern base bodies)
Be subtle and celestiall sweete accord (By subtle and celes-
   tial sweet accord)
Then greate is Ticho who by this his booke (Then great is
   Tycho who by this his book)
Commandement doth ouer these commanders brooke.
   (Allows commandment over these commanders.)

Another on the same

The glorious globe of heauenlie matter made (The glorious
   globe made of heavenly matter)
Containing ten celestiall circles faire (Containing ten fair
   celestial circles)
Where shining stares in glistering graithe arraide (Where
   shining stars, arrayed in glittering attire,)
Most pleasantly are poudered here and thair (Most pleasantly are powdered here and there)
Where euerie planet hath his own repaire (Where every
   planet has his own place)
And christall house, a whirling wheill in rounde (And
   crystal house, a wheel whirling 'round)
Whose calme aspects or forward does declaire (Whose
   appearance, whether calm or angry, declares)
Gods minde to blisse great kingdoms or confounde (God's
   mind, whether to bless great kingdoms or confound
   them)

Then if yow list to see on earthlie grounde (Then, if you
    wish to see from the earthly ground)
There ordour, course, and influence appeare (Their order,
    proper progress, and influence)
Looke Tichoes tooles, there finelie shall be founde (Look to
    Tycho's tool, where beautifully shall be found)
Each planet dancing in his propre spheare (Each planet
    dancing in his proper sphere)
There fire diuine into his house remaine (Divine fire will
    remain in the house)
Whome sommerlie his booke doth here containe. (That
    wisely contains his book.)

Another on the same

What foolish Phaeton did presume in pride (What foolish
    Phaeton did in pride presume)
Yea more what great Apollo takes in hand (Yea, more, what
    great Apollo takes in hand)
Who does the course of glistring Phoebus guide (He who
    guides glittering Phoebus along its path)
Thou does performe that rules eache firie brand (You
    perform, by ruling each fiery brand)
Then greater art thou then Apollo cleare (So, you are
    greater than bright Apollo)
As thy Vranias eldest fostre deare. (You are Urania's dear
    eldest foster child.)

(VI/I, 2015)

APPENDIX 2

The Phoenix and the Turtle

Let the bird of loudest lay,
On the sole Arabian tree,
Herald sad and trumpet be,
To whose sound chaste wings obey.

But thou, shrieking harbinger,
Foul pre-currer of the fiend,
Augur of the fever's end,
To this troop come thou not near.

From this session interdict
Every fowl of tyrant wing,
Save the eagle, feather'd king:
Keep the obsequy so strict.

Let the priest in surplice white,
That defunctive music can,
Be the death-divining swan,
Lest the requiem lack his right.

And thou, treble-dated crow,
That thy sable gender mak'st
With the breath thou giv'st and tak'st,
'Mongst our mourners shalt thou go.

Here the anthem doth commence:
Love and constancy is dead;
Phoenix and the turtle fled
In a mutual flame from hence.

So they lov'd, as love in twain
Had the essence but in one;
Two distincts, division none:
Number there in love was slain.

Hearts remote, yet not asunder;
Distance, and no space was seen
'Twixt the turtle and his queen;
But in them it were a wonder.

So between them love did shine,
That the turtle saw his right
Flaming in the phoenix' sight:
Either was the other's mine.

Property was thus appall'd,
That the self was not the same;
Single nature's double name
Neither two nor one was call'd.

Reason, in itself confounded,
Saw division grow together;
To themselves yet either-neither,
Simple were so well compounded

That it cried how true a twain
Seemeth this concordant one!
Love hath reason, reason none
If what parts can so remain.

Whereupon it made this threne
To the phoenix and the dove,
Co-supreme and stars of love;
As chorus to their tragic scene.

THRENOS.

Beauty, truth, and rarity.
Grace in all simplicity,
Here enclos'd in cinders lie.

Death is now the phoenix' nest;
And the turtle's loyal breast
To eternity doth rest,

Leaving no posterity:–
'Twas not their infirmity,
It was married chastity.

Truth may seem, but cannot be:
Beauty brag, but 'tis not she;
Truth and beauty buried be.

To this urn let those repair
That are either true or fair;
For these dead birds sigh a prayer.

APPENDIX 3
Timeline

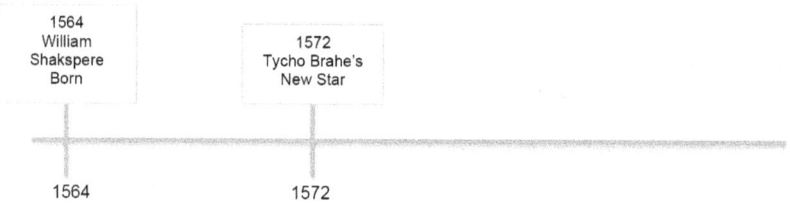

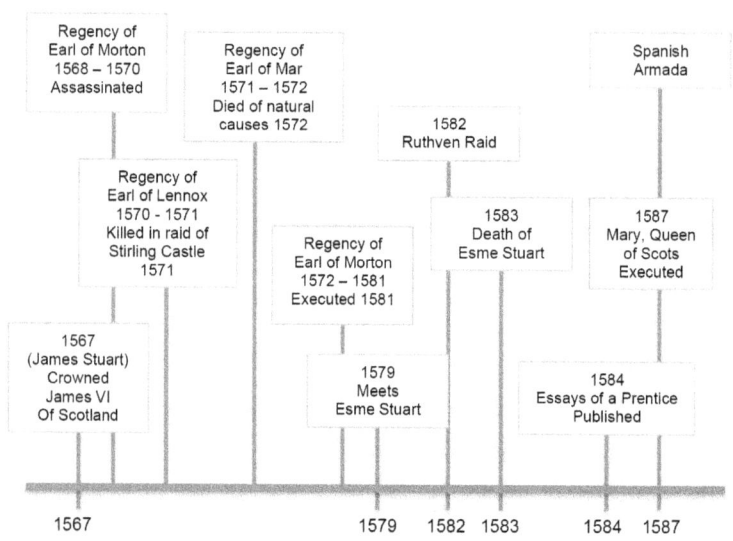

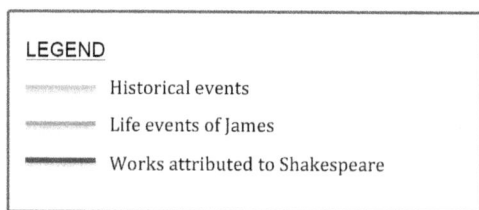

Appendix 3 | Timeline   171

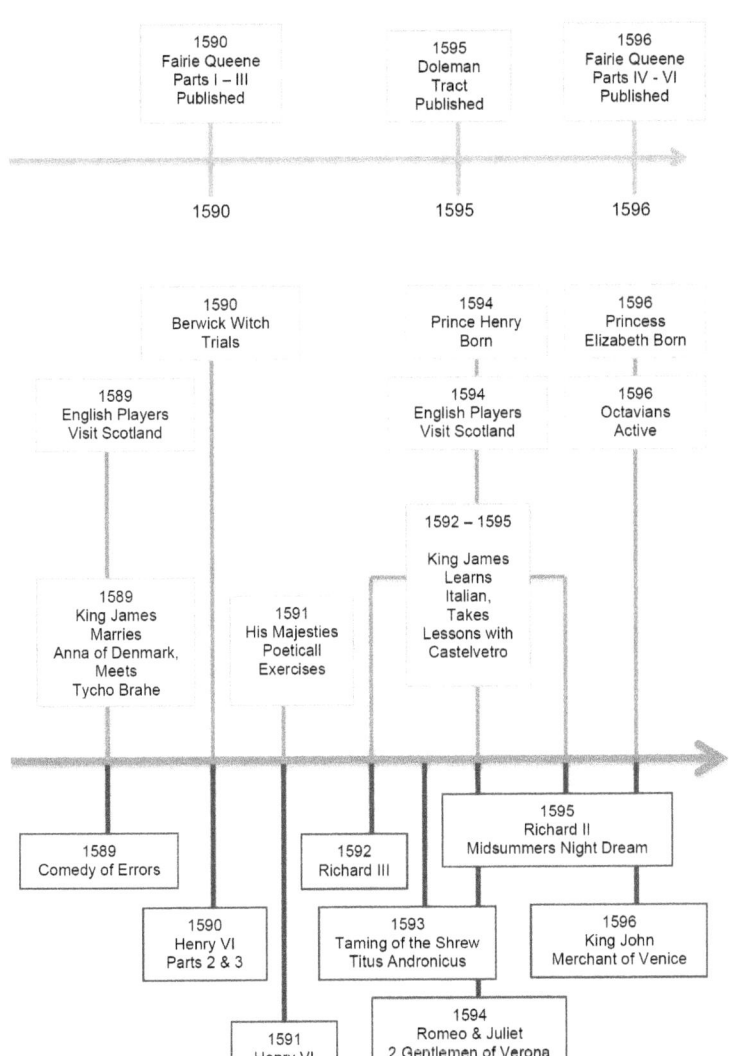

1598
Death of
William Cecil
1601
Essex Rebellion
Death of
Tycho Brahe
1604
Hampton Court
Conference
1598
1601
1604

1601
English Players
Visit Scotland
1600
Prince Charles
Born
1605
Gunpowder Plot
1597
Daemonologie
Published
1599
Basilkon
Doron
1603
James VI of Scotland
Becomes
King James I of England
1598
True Lawe
Published
1600
Gowrie Plot
1597
Henry IV
Parts 1 & 2
1599
12th Night
As you Like It
Julius Caesar
1602
Alls Well That
Ends Well
1604
Othello
Measure for Measure
1600
Hamlet
Merry Wives of Windsor
1603
No Works
Written
1605
King Lear
Macbeth
1598
Henry V
Much Ado About Nothing
1601
Troilus & Cressida
Poem: Phoenix & The Turtle

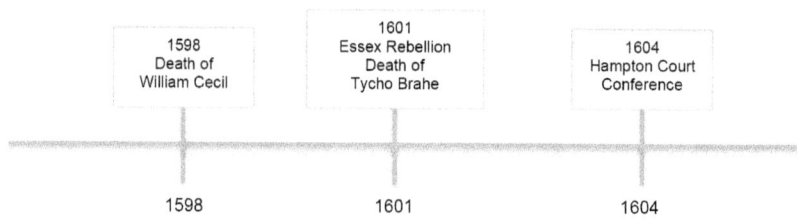

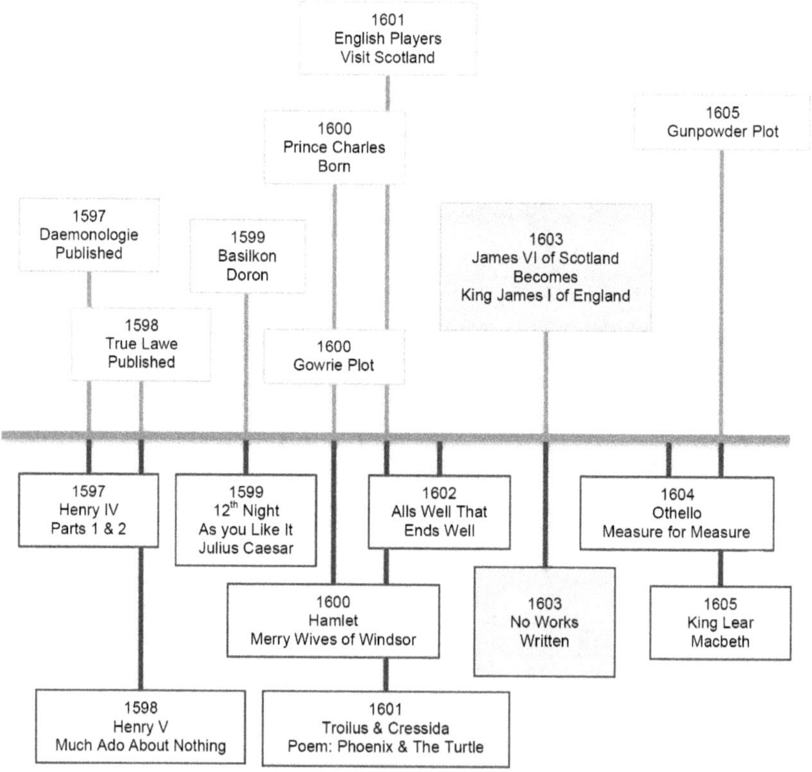

Appendix 3 | Timeline 173

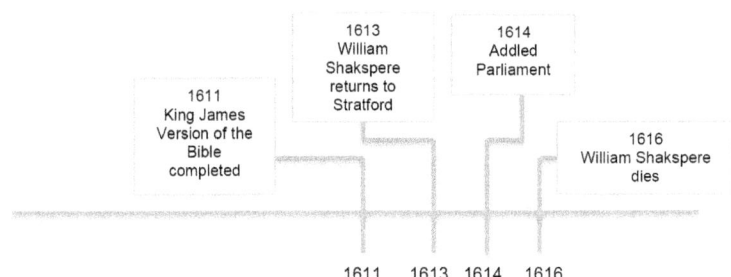

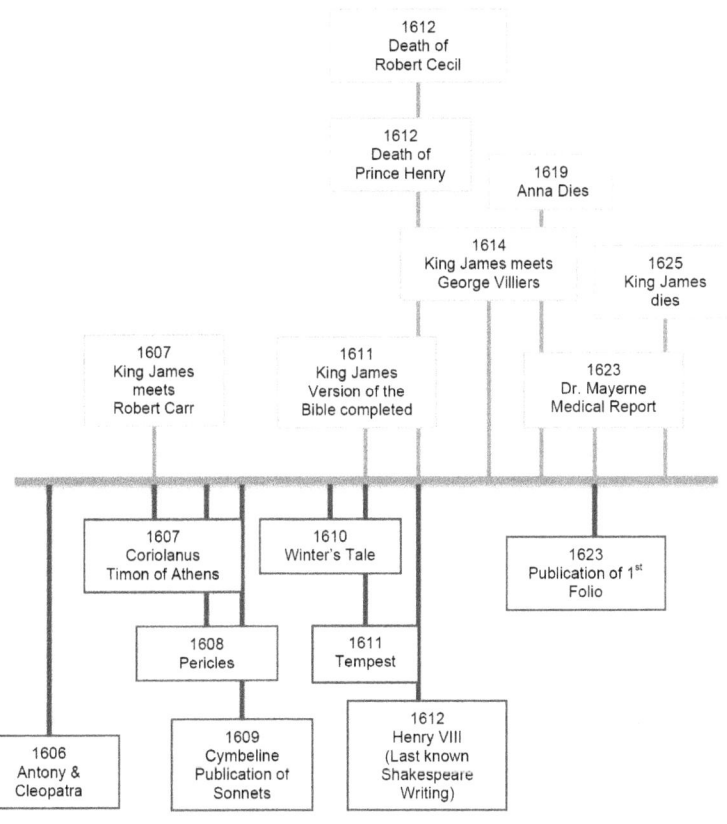

Bibliography

Addled Parliament. (n.d.). In *Wikipedia*. Retrieved July 28, 2015, from https://en.wikipedia.org/wiki/Addled_Parliament

Akrigg, G. P. V. (1984). *Letters of King James VI & I.* Oakley, CA: University of California Press.

Argumentum ad hominem. (n.d.). In *RationalWiki*. Retrieved April 20, 2015, from www.rationalwiki.org/wiki/Ad_hominem

Bawcutt, P. (2001). James VI/I's Castalian band: A modern myth. *The Scottish Historical Review*, 80(210), 251–259.

Bergeron, D. M. (1999). *King James and letters of homoerotic desire.* Iowa CIty, IA: Univerity of Iowa Press.

Black, M. W. (1955). *A New Variorum Edition of Shakespeare: The Life and Death of Richard the Second.* Philadelphia, PA: J.B. Lippincott.

Cecil, W. (1584). Certain precepts for the well ordering of a man's life. At *Hamlet: The Undiscovered Country*. Retrieved from www.princehamlet.com/burghley.html

Chaplin, C. (1964). *My autobiography.* London, UK: The Bodley Head.

Craigie, J. (1950). Last poems of James VI. *The Scottish Historical Review*, 29(108), 134–142.

Croft, P. (2003). *King James.* London, UK: Palgrave Macmillan.

Desmond, J. F. (2011, July 6). Shakespeare: Closet Catholic?. *National Catholic Register*. Retrieved from http://www.ncregister.com/daily-news/shakespeare-closet-catholic

Doran, S. (2006). James VI and the English succession. In R. A. Houlbrooke (ed.), *James VI and I: Ideas, authority, and government.* Aldershot, UK: Ashgate.

Dragsholm Castle. (n.d.). In *Wikipedia*. Retrieved May 26, 2015, from www.en.wikipedia.org/wiki/Dragsholm_Castle

Emmett, R. J. (2010, September). *Anglo-Scottish succession tracts during the late Elizabethan period, 1595–1603.* Retrieved from eTheses Repository, http://etheses.bham.ac.uk/1392/

Fitzgerald, J. (1999). Know ye not this parable? The Oxford-Du Bartas connection. *The Oxfordian*, 76–116.

Garber, M. (2004). *Shakespeare after all.* New York, NY: Pantheon Books.

George Mason University. (2015, May 30). *Concordance of Shakespeare's complete works.* Retrieved from www.opensourceshakespeare.org/concordance

Greenspan, S. (2010, November 15). *11 pieces of evidence that Shakespeare was gay.* Retrieved from www.11points.com/Books/11_Pieces_Of_Evidence_That_Shakespeare_Was_Gay

Greer, G. (2007). *Shakespeare's wife.* Toronto, Canada: McClelland & Stewart.

Herman, P. (2001). Authorship and the royal "I:" King James VI/I and the politics of monarchic verse. *Renaissance Quarterly, 54*(4), 1495–1530.

Jack, R. (1970). William Fowler and Italian literature. *The Modern Language Review, 65*(3), 481–492.

James VI and I. (n.d.). *Sonnets by James VI.* Retrieved from www.arts.gla.ac.uk/STELLA/STARN/poetry/SONNETS/james.htm

James VI and I. (1597). *Daemonologie.* Edinburgh, Scotland: Robert Waldegrave.

James VI and I. (1603). *Basilikon doron or his majesties instructions to his dearest sonne, Henry the prince.* London, England.

James VI and I. (1604). *A Counter-blaste to Tobacco.* London: Unwin Brothers.

James VI and I and the English Parliament. (n.d.). in *Wikipedia.* Retrieved July 28, 2015, from https://en.wikipedia.org/wiki/James_VI_and_I_and_the_English_Parliament

Lawrence Fletcher. (n.d.). In *Wikipedia.* Retrieved September 7, 2013, from www.en.wikipedia.org/wiki/Lawrence_Fletcher

Lee, M. (1990). *Great Britain's Solomon.* Urbana, IL: University of Illinois Press.

Lord High Admiral of Scotland. (n.d.). In *Wikipedia.* Retrieved January 14, 2014, from www.en.wikipedia.org/wiki/Lord_High_Admiral_of_Scotland

Mabillard, A. (2000a, August 19). *Representations of kingship and power in Shakespeare's second tetralogy.* Retrieved from www.shakespeare-online.com/essays/power.html

Mabillard, A. (2000b, August 20). *Shakespeare's sources for* The Merchant of Venice. Retrieved from www.shakespeare-online.com/sources/merchantsources.html

Maley, W., & Murphy, A. (2004). *Shakespeare and Scotland*. Manchester, UK: Manchester University Press.

Mary, Queen of Scots. (n.d.). In *Wikipedia*. Retrieved June 2, 2015, from www.en.wikipedia.org/wiki/Mary,_Queen_of_Scots

McIlwain, C. H. (1918). *The political works of James I*. Cambridge, MA: Harvard University Press.

Narrative and dramatic sources of all Shakespeare's works. (2008). At *The Bard of Avon: Shakespeare in Stratford-upon-Avon*. Retrieved from www.shakespeare-w.com/english/shakespeare/source.html

No fear Shakespeare. (2015). Available at http://nfs.sparknotes.com

Norton, R. (2012, January 9). *Queen James and his courtiers*. Retrieved from http://rictornorton.co.uk/jamesi.htm

Order of succession. (n.d.). In *Wikipedia*. Retrieved April 2, 2015, from www.en.wikipedia.org/wiki/Order_of_succession

Osiander, Andreas. (2008). In *Complete Dictionary of Scientific Biography*. Retrieved from http://www.encyclopedia.com/topic/Andreas_Osiander.aspx

Peck, L. L. (1991). *The mental world of the Jacobean court*. Cambridge, UK: Cambridge Universtiy Press.

Personal relationships of James VI and I. (n.d.). In *Wikipedia*. Retrieved May 13, 2015, from www.en.wikipedia.org/wiki/Personal_relationships_of_James_VI_and_I

Peters, T., Garrard, P., Ganesan, V., & Stephenson, J. (2012). The nature of King James VI/I's medical conditions: New approaches to the diagnosis. *History of Psychiatry, 23*(3), 277–290.

Petrina, A. (2007). The travels of ideology: Niccolo Machiavelli at the court of James VI. *The Modern Language Review*, 102(4), 947–959.

Price, D. (2001). *Shakespeare's unorthodox biography*. Westport, CT: Greenwood Press.

Rhodes, N., Richards, J., & Marshall, J. (2003). *King James VI and I: Selected writings*. Burlington, VT: Ashgate.

Rickard, J. (2007). *Authorship and authority: The writings of James VI and I*. Manchester, UK: Manchester University Press.

Rubbo, M., & McDonald, P. (Directors). (2001). Much ado about something [Television series episode]. In *Frontline*. London, UK: BBC Studios.

Rudd, A. (2013, February 20). Prince Philip quotes: Relive 65 classic gaffes as Duke of Edinburgh celebrates 65th wedding anniversary. *Mirror*. Retrieved from http://www.mirror.co.uk/news/uk-news/prince-philip-quotes-relive-65-1445185

Schama, S. (Writer), & BBC (Director). (2012). Hollow crowns [Television series episode]. In *Simon Schama's Shakespeare: Hollow crowns*. London, UK: BBC Studios.

Shakespeare authorship. (n.d.). In *RationalWiki*. Retrieved June 4, 2015, from www.rationalwiki.org/wiki/Shakespeare_authorship

Shakespeare Authorship Coalition. (2015, June 6). *Declaration of reasonable doubt about the identity of William Shakespeare*. Retrieved from www.doubtaboutwill.org/declaration

Smith, R. E. (2009, February 2). Did James VI of Scotland write Ur-Hamlet? [Msg 1]. Message posted to www.online-literature.com/forums/showthread.php?41482-Did-James-VI-of-Scotland-write-Ur-Hamlet

SN 1572. (n.d.). In *Wikipedia*. Retrieved June 12, 2015, from www.en.wikipedia.org/wiki/SN_1572

Stewart, A. (2011). *The cradle king: A life of James VI & I*. New York, NY: Random House.

Trevor-Roper, H. (1962, November). What's in a name? *Réalités* [English edition], 41–43.

Twain, M. (1991). Is Shakespeare dead? (From my autobiography). In C. Neider (ed.), *The Complete Essays of Mark Twain* (pp. 407–454). New York, NY: Harper & Brothers Publishers.

University College London. (2007, March 22). Was Shakespeare lame? *UCL Media Relations*. Retrieved from www.ucl.ac.uk/media/library/Shakespeare

Usher, P. (2010). *Shakespeare and the dawn of modern science*. Amherst, NY: Cambria Press.

Williams, K., Holmes, F., Kemper, S., Marquis, J. (2003). Written language clues to cognitive changes of aging: An analysis of the letters of King James VI/I. *Journal of Gerontology: Psychological Sciences*, 58B(1), 42–44.

Wilson, D. H. (1959). *King James VI and I*. London, UK: Cape.

Wilson, L., & Wilson, L. (Directors). (2012). *Last Will. & testament* [Television program].

Wormald, J. (1983). James VI and I: Two kings or one? *History*, 68(223), 187–209.

Wormald, J. (2000). "'Tis true I am a cradle king": The view from the throne. In J. Goodare & M. Lynch (eds.), *The reign of James VI* (pp. 241–256). East Linton, UK: Tuckwell Press.

X, M., & Haley, A. (1965). *The autobiography of Malcolm X*. New York, NY: Grove Press.

Index

'30' (code number), 75, 145–146
Act against Seditious Words . . . against the Queen's . . . Majesty, 55
Act of Association, 57–58
Addled Parliament, 83
Almagest, 46–48, 146–149
'Ane Metaphoricall Invention of a Tragedie Called Phoenix', 39–40, 130, 150, 159
Anna, of Denmark *see* Anne, Queen
Anne, Queen, xvi, 43–48, 50, 52, 64, 110, 125–126, 129–130, 152
Anniversary Days Observation Act, 84
Astronomy/Cosmology, 17–18, 28–30, 32, 46–48, 146–149, 158
Augustus, Caesar, 94–95
Aviz, House of, 59

B Cassiopeeiae *see* SN1572/ Supernova of 1572

Bacon, Sir Francis, 4–6, 97
Basilikon Doron, 61, 67–68, 88, 102, 159
Battle of Bosworth Field, 21, 103, 120–121
Battle of Carberry Hill, 25–26, 52
Battle of Lepanto, 27–28, 53–54, 151
Beaufort, John, 21
Beaumont, Francis, 14
Bergen, 25
Bishop of Zealand *see* Mathias, Povel
Bolingbroke, Henry *see* Henry IV, King of England
Bothwell, 4th Earl of *see* Hepburn, James
Bothwell, 5th Earl of *see* Stewart, Francis
Brahe, Tycho, 28–31, 46–48, 102, 146–149, 155–156, 159, 163–165
Britain, 70, 82–83, 95, 136, 153–154, 158, 160
Bruce, Edward, Lord Kinloss, 75, 144

179

Buchanan, George, 31–32, 46, 66, 94, 122–123
Burghley, Lord *see* Cecil, William

Carr, Robert, 1st Earl of Sommerset, 84–87, 92
Castalian Band, 36–39, 107, 158
Castelvetro, Giacomo, 63–64, 68, 104–105, 126–127, 129, 134, 159
Cecil, Robert, 1st Earl of Salisbury, 71–77, 79, 84–85, 87, 91, 94, 115, 143, 160
Cecil, William, Lord Burghley, 71, 143
Chaplin, Charlie, 1, 7, 9, 11
Chapman, George, 14, 113
Charles I, King of England, 50, 60, 81, 83, 87, 93
Charles V, Holy Roman Emperor, 27, 68
Cinthio *see* Giraldi, Giovanni
Civil war, 18–24, 55, 77–78, 81, 120–122, 128, 137
Commedia dell'arte, 42, 105, 134
Comedy of Errors, 105, 125, 127
Common people/Commoners, 1–2, 4, 93–94, 132. *See also* House of Commons
Confederate Lords, 25–26
Copenhagen, 22, 26, 45. *See also* Denmark
Copernicus, Nicholas/Copernicanism/Copernican theory, 46–47, 102, 146–149
Cosmology *see* Astronomy/Cosmology
Counterblaste to Tobacco, 81

Cymbeline, 104, 136, 146, 154, 160
Cyprus, 27, 151

Daemonologie, 65–66, 102
Danes/The Danish *see* Denmark
De Jure Regni apud Scotos, 31
De Mayerne, Theodore, 89–90
De natis ultra mare, 57
De nova et nullius aevi memoria prius visa stella, 29, 46
De Revolutionibus orbium coelestium, 46, 147–149
De Vere, Edward, 17th Earl of Oxford, 5, 98, 104, 118
Dekker, Thomas, 14
Denmark, 22, 26, 28–31, 43–48, 51–52, 102, 104, 132, 138–148, 155, 159
Deposition scene, xiv, 73–74, 133
Devereux, Robert, 2nd Earl of Essex, xiv, 69–75, 77, 115, 133, 144
Devil, the *see* Satan
Dickens, Charles, 6, 9
Digges, Leonard (scientist), 147–148
Digges, Leonard (writer), 8
Digges, Thomas, 147–148
Divine right of kings/Divine right theory, 66–68, 121, 133–134, 158, 160
Doleman tract, 60–61, 121
Don John of Austria *see* John of Austria
Douglas, James, 4th Earl of Morton, 34, 131
Dragsholm Castle, 26

Du Bartas, Guillaume de Salluste, 36–38, 54, 118, 132
Duessa, 63, 145

Edinburgh, 25, 34, 40, 49, 65, 75, 126–127
Edmund of Langley, 1st Duke of York, 20–21. *See also* York, House of
Edward the Black Prince, 19
Edward III, King of England, 18–21
Edward IV, King of England, 21
Edward VI, King of England, 56
Elective monarchy, 60, 139, 144
Elizabeth, Queen of Bohemia (daughter of James VI/I), 50, 83
Elizabeth I, Queen of England, xiii–xviii, 15, 21, 24, 40–41, 48, 54–62, 69–79, 93, 100, 119–122, 133, 137–138, 142–143, 159
Elk, Tycho Brahe's *see* Moose, Tycho Brahe's
Elsinore, xvi, 45, 138, 140, 144, 159
English (language), 5–6, 12, 32, 36, 54, 80, 100, 105, 111, 151, 158
Epistemon *see Daemonologie*
Erskine, John, Earl of Mar, 75, 144
Essayes of a Prentise, in the Divine Art of Poesie, 38–40, 159
Essex, Earl of *see* Devereux, Robert
Essex Rebellion, xiv, 69–75, 77, 133, 144, 160
Euphuism, 118–119

'Fair youth' sonnets, 112, 117. *See also* 'procreation' sonnets

Faerie Queene, The, 62–63, 145
Fawkes, Guy, 83–84. *See also* Gunpowder Plot
Field, Richard, 40, 150, 159–160
Fiorentino, Giovanni, 134
First Folio, 8, 89, 105, 117, 121–123, 160
Fletcher, John, 14, 114
Fletcher, Lawrence/Laurence, 48–49, 159
Fowler, William, 36–39, 45, 104
France, 18–22, 35, 37–38, 131, 135–136, 139, 140, 143
Francis II, King of France, 22–23, 142
Frederick II, King of Denmark, 26, 29, 43
French (language), 3, 32, 54, 118, 158

General Assembly of Scotland, 81–82
Gentry/landed gentry, 59, 128, 137
Geocentrism *see* Ptolemy, Claudius
Geoheliocentrism *see* Brahe, Tycho
Gertrude, xvi, 116, 138–145
Ghosts, 26, 52, 86, 138–142, 148. *See also* Supernatural/Occult
Giraldi, Giovanni, 105
Glamis, Master of, 35
Globe Theatre, 42, 73
Gloriana *see Faeirie Queene, The*
Gordon, George, 6th Earl of Huntly, 42
Gowrie, 1st Earl of *see* Ruthven, William
Gowrie, 3rd Earl of *see* Ruthven, John

Gowrie plot/Conspiracy/Mystery, 68–69, 84
Gowrie regime, 35
Great Britain *see* Britain
Greek (language), 32, 122–123, 158
Greene, Robert, 14, 133
'Gudeman of Ballengeich' *see* James V, King of Scots
Guildenstern *see* Rosencrantz and Guildenstern
Gunpowder Plot, 83–84, 110

Hamlet, xvi, 12, 65, 104, 125, 138–149, 159
Hampton Court Conference, 80, 152, 160
Hathaway, Anne, 2
Haunting/Haunted castles *see* ghosts
Heliocentrism *see* Copernicus, Nicholas
Helsingor *see* Elsinore
Heminges, John and Condell, William, 8
Henry IV, King of England, 20, 58, 133–135
Henry IV, King of France, 24, 43
Henry IV Pts 1&2 (plays), 121, 134–135, 159
Henry V, King of England, 20, 121, 135–136
Henry V (play), 121, 135–137, 159
Henry VI, King of England, 20–21, 128
Henry VI, Pts 1–3 (plays), 119–120, 125, 128–129, 159
Henry VII, King of England, 21, 23, 56–59, 94–95, 103–104, 120–121, 129, 158
Henry VIII, King of England, 21, 56–58, 70
Henry VIII (play), 43, 114–115, 120, 160
Henry Frederick, Prince of Wales, 50, 60, 67, 74, 84–87, 107, 160
Hepburn, James, 4th Earl of Bothwell, 22–26, 51, 142
Herbert, Phillip, 1st Earl of Montgomery, 116–117
Herbert, William, 3rd Earl of Pembroke, 117
Hereditary monarchy *see* primogeniture
Heywood, Thomas, 14
His Maiesties Poeticall Exercises at Vacant Houres, 52–54,
Holy League, 27–28. See also Venice
Homoeroticism/Homosexuality, 17, 39, 108–109, 116–117, 150–151, 157. See also favourites
House of Commons, 81–82. See also parliament
House of Lords, 81, 83–84. See also parliament
Hudson, Robert and Thomas, 36–37, 107
Hundred Years' War, 18, 20
Hunting, 34, 68, 77, 91, 105–107, 158
Huntly, Earl of *see* Gordon, George
Huntly wedding masque, 42–43, 102, 105, 159
Hven, island of, 29, 46, 159

Iago, 151–152
Il Pecorone (The Simpleton), 134
'Incomparable pair of brethren' *see* Herbert, Phillip *and* Herbert, William
Isabella Clara Eugenia, Infanta of Spain, 60–61, 128
Italian (language), 5, 32, 37, 63, 68, 104–105, 126, 129, 134
Italy, 5, 37, 42, 63, 104–105, 111, 126–127, 129, 159

James V, King of Scots, 57, 136–137
James VI/I, King of Great Britain (self-proclaimed)
  attitude toward women of, 50–51, 129–130, 157
  claim to English throne of, 41, 43, 54–62, 66–67, 70–78, 95, 120–122, 128–129, 134–137
  education of, 31–33, 63, 102, 157–159
  finances of, 64–65, 78, 82, 91–92, 107–108
  health of, 87–90, 160
  lameness/legs/lower limb disability of, 89, 112, 157
  poetry and/of, 36–40, 52–54, 67–68, 88, 102, 118
  religion and, 66–67, 80, 109–111
  secretiveness of, 99, 153
  sexuality of, 33–34, 39, 50, 84–87, 90, 108–109, 116–117, 150–151, 157
  theatre and, 42–43, 48–49, 78–79, 102

John of Austria/Don John of Austria, 27–28, 54
John of Gaunt, 1st Duke of Lancaster, 19–21, 58–59, 103, 114. *See also* Lancaster, House of
Jones, Inigo, 42–43
Jonson, Ben, xiv, 8, 14, 43, 88, 113, 122–123, 149
Julius Caesar, 1, 104, 122, 137, 159

Kepler, Johannes, 30
King James *see* Stuart, James
King Lear, xviii, 112, 132, 136, 153–154, 160
Kirk (Scottish church), 49, 62
Kyd, Thomas, xiv, 14
Krongborg castle *see* Elsinore

Lady Macbeth, 116
Lancaster, House of, 18–21, 57–59, 61, 95, 103–104, 120–121
Lancastrians *see* Lancaster, House of
Latin (language), 31–32, 84, 95, 122–123, 158
Law, study of, 32, 158
Lepanto (poem), 53–54, 151. *See also* Battle of Lepanto
Lionel of Antwerp, 1st Duke of Clarence, 19, 21
"Little Beagle" *see* Cecil, Robert
Lord Chamberlain's Men, 2, 48–49, 73, 78–79, 119–120, 159. *See also* King's Men
Lords Enterprisers, 34–35

Lodge, Thomas, 14
London, 1–2, 14, 40, 49–50, 71, 73–78, 80, 95, 119, 126, 159
Looney, J. Thomas *see* Shakespeare Identified
Love's Labour's Lost, 104, 132, 146
Lyly, John, 14, 119

Macbeth, xviii, 31, 114, 154–155
Machiavelli, Niccolo, 37, 39, 104
Makar, 36
Malcolm X *see* X, Malcolm
Male primogeniture *see* primogeniture
Marlowe, Christopher, xiv, 4–5, 14, 113
Marston, John, 14, 113
Mary, Queen of Scots, xvi, xviii, 22–26, 31–32, 40–41, 54–55, 57–60, 63, 107, 115–116, 142–143, 145
Masque *see* Huntly wedding masque
Mathias, Povel, Bishop of Zealand, 45, 101
Measure for Measure, 105, 152–153, 160
Medicine, study of, 32, 45, 158
Merchant of Venice, 104, 133–134, 146
Middleton, Thomas, 14
Midsummer Night's Dream, 43, 133
Military science, 32
Mongomerie, Alexander, 36
Moose, Tycho Brahe's, 30, 48
'Mr. W.H.', 117
Music/Musicians, 36, 42–43, 107, 111, 158

Nashe, Thomas, 14
Navarre, 38, 43, 132
Nine Years' War, 70, 72
North Berwick witch trials, 50–52, 65
Norway, 25, 45, 52, 139

Occult *see* Supernatural/Occult
Octavians, 64–65, 108, 133
Osiander, Andreas, 149
Othello, xviii, 104–105, 151–152
Ottoman Empire, 27–28, 53–54, 151
Oxford, Earl of *see* De Vere, Edward

Parker, William, 4th Baron Monteagle, 84
Parliament, 55, 58, 73–74, 81–84
Persons/Parsons, Robert, 60–61. *See also* Doleman tract
Petrarch, 37, 39, 104–105
Philip II, King of Spain, 27, 55, 61, 68, 144
Phillip III, King of Spain, 144
Philomathes *see* Daemonologie
Phoenix and the Turtle, 149–150, 160, 167–169. *See also* 'Ane Metaphoricall Invention of a Tragedie Called Phoenix'
Poland, 140–141, 147, 149
Primogeniture, 18–21, 54–61, 134–135, 144, 160
'Procreation sonnets', 117, 158. *See also* 'fair youth' sonnets
Prospero, 116, 155–156
Ptolemy, Claudius, 46–48, 146–149

Puritans, 14, 80, 110, 152–153, 158, 160

Rerum Scoticarum Historia, 31
Resistance Theory, 31, 60, 66
Richard II, King of England, 19–20, 132
Richard II (play), xiv, 73–74, 114, 121, 132–134, 159
Richard III, King of England, 21, 59, 120–121, 129
Richard III (play), 114, 116, 119–120, 128–129, 159
Richard, 3rd Duke of York, 20–21
Rizzio, David, 23–24, 151–152
Rome, 104, 131, 137
Romeo and Juliet, 43, 104, 130–132, 159
Rozencrantz and Guildenstern, 140–141, 144, 147
Rozenkrantz, Eric, 25–26
Rosenkrantz Tower, 26
Ruthven, Alexander, 68–69
Ruthven, John, 3rd Earl of Gowrie, 68–69
Ruthven, William, 1st Earl of Gowrie, 34–35, 69
Ruthven Raid, 34–36, 131

Salic law, 135
Salisbury, Earl of *see* Cecil, Robert
Sampson, 51–52
Satan, Prince of Darkness, 50–52, 62, 65
Schama, Simon, xiii–xvi, 142
Scots (language), 32, 36–38, 158
Sermon on the Mount, 152–153, 92

Seton (hereditary royal armour-bearers), 155
Shakespeare Authorship Coalition, 10
Shakespeare Birthplace Trust, 10
Shakespeare Identified, 5, 97–111, 160–161
Shakespeare's sonnets, 12, 15, 108, 112, 117, 156, 157
Shakspere, Hamnet, 2, 138
Shakspere, Susanna and Judith, 2–3, 11–12
Shakspere, Willliam, 2–3, 7–14
Skottefruen *see* Throndsen, Anna
SN1572/Supernova of 1572, 17–18, 28–29, 138, 148
Solomon, King of Israel, 24, 94–95
Sommerset, Earl of *see* Carr, Robert
Sonnet, 12, 15, 37, 48, 52, 67–68, 88, 102, 105, 157. *See also* Shakespeare's sonnets
Southampton, Earl of *see* Wriothesley, Henry
Spain, 27, 55, 59, 61, 70, 72, 93, 144
Spanish (language), 32, 152, 158
Spanish Armada, xiv, 55, 70
Spenser, Edmund, 14, 62–63, 145
Sport *see* Hunting
Stanley, Anne, Countess of Castlehaven, 58, 128
Stanley, Margaret, Countess of Derby, 58
Star catalogue, 29–30, 46–48, 156
Stewart, Esmé *see* Stuart, Esmé
Stewart, Francis, 5th Earl of Bothwell, 51–52
Stewart, Henry, Lord Darnley, xvi, 23–25, 142, 151

Stigma of print, 4
Stirling Castle, 27, 51, 137
Storms/Tempests, 17, 25, 45, 52, 155–156, 159
Stratford-upon-Avon, xv, 1, 2–3, 7–8, 11–13, 40, 159
Stratfordians/Stratfordian position, 7–12, 119–120
Stuart, Arabella, 37, 57–57, 61–62, 76–77, 128–129, 137
Stuart, Esmé, 1st Duke of Lennox, 33–36, 39, 42, 86, 92, 109, 130–132, 150–151, 158–160
Stuart, James *see* James VI/I
Stuart/Stewart, House of, 76, 103
Succession tract, 56–62, 66, 120–122, 160(n)
Supernatural/Occult, 32, 156, 158. See also ghosts *and* witchcraft/witches
Supernova *see* SN1572/Supernova of 1572

Taming of the Shrew, 104–105, 125, 129–130
Tempest, The, xviii, 43, 155–156
Tempests *see* Storms/Tempests
Theology, 32, 45, 102, 109
Third Succession Act, 58
Throndsen, Anna "Skottefruen", 22, 25–26
'To the Memory of My Beloved the Author', 122
True Law of Free Monarchies, 61, 66–67, 159–160
Tudor, Henry, Duke of Richmond *see* Henry VII, King of England

Tudor, House of, 21, 23, 54–59, 76
Tudor, Margaret, 23, 56–58
Tudor, Mary, 58
Turks *see* Ottoman Empire
Twain, Mark, 7, 9, 11, 97
Tycho's Supernova *see* SN1572/Supernova of 1572

Vautrollier, Thomas, 40, 159
Venice, 27, 53–54, 63, 104–105, 133–134, 151
Venus and Adonis, 5, 40, 159
Verona, 37, 104, 132
Vienna, 63, 152–153
Villiers, George, 1st Duke of Buckingham, 86–87, 115

Walsingham, Sir Francis, 63
Wars of the Roses, 18–21, 120–121
Weddings, 17, 42–45, 116–117, 157
Weldon, Anthony, 90
Witchcraft/Witches, 17, 50–52, 65, 158. See also Supernatural/Occult
The Workes of the Most High and Mightie Prince, 88
Wriothesley, Henry, 3rd Earl of Southampton, 73–74

X, Malcolm, xiv, xvii, 5–6, 9

York, House of, 18–21, 59, 95, 120–121
Young, Peter, 32–33

About the Author

Ian Stockdale holds a B.A. (Political Science) from Simon Fraser University. Formerly employed representing the employment interests of academics, he currently lives as a masterless man. Ian lives with his family in Burnaby, British Columbia, Canada.

The author emerging from a phonebox, London, 2010

www.ingramcontent.com/pod-product-compliance
Lightning Source LLC
Chambersburg PA
CBHW050536300426
44113CB00012B/2121